COOKING
FOR THE
FREEZER

BY MYRA WALDO

COOKING FOR THE FREEZER

DINER'S CLUB COOKBOOK

COMPLETE BOOK OF ORIENTAL COOKING

SERVE AT ONCE: THE SOUFFLÉ COOKBOOK

BEER AND GOOD FOOD

1001 WAYS TO PLEASE A HUSBAND

THE SLENDERELLA COOKBOOK

DINING OUT IN ANY LANGUAGE

THE COMPLETE ROUND-THE-WORLD COOKBOOK

CO-AUTHOR

THE MOLLY GOLDBERG JEWISH COOKBOOK
With Gertrude Berg

TRAVEL BOOKS

MYRA WALDO'S TRAVEL GUIDE TO EUROPE

NEW HORIZONS, USA

BY MYRA WALDO

COOKING

FOR THE

FREEZER

DOLPHIN BOOKS

DOUBLEDAY & COMPANY, INC., GARDEN CITY, NEW YORK

Dolphin Books Edition: 1975
Originally published by Doubleday
& Company, Inc., in 1960

CONTENTS

COOKING
FOR THE
FREEZER

INTRODUCTION

Much has been written about freezing raw foods, but not about cooked foods. Cooking specifically for the freezer is a fine art. Of course it's a great convenience to pop leftovers into the freezer, but when you're preparing foods with the definite purpose of freezing for future use, the full flavor of the dish can be retained only by following special procedures.

A freezer is no longer a luxury, because of its usefulness, nor is it impossible to fit into the smallest kitchen. Manufacturers have taken into consideration the decrease of floor space in new construction and have produced freezers as small as a 2 cubic-foot wall type, on up to 18-foot shelf freezers.

With a freezer, special holiday and company meals may be prepared well in advance, so that on the day itself you can relax and enjoy being with your guests. Also, having a series of cooked, ready dishes in the freezer gives you a delightful sense of security; no longer can unexpected guests throw your plans into confusion. On lazy or busy days, one of those specially prepared frozen dishes can provide your family with a delicious meal with the least possible effort on your part. Take advantage of sales in your supermarket, but cook the foods rather than freeze them raw.

Not all foods freeze equally well, and therefore only those dishes which reconstitute satisfactorily after freezing should be considered. Also, and this is vitally important with meat or fish dishes, the additional cooking time necessary to reheat the frozen dish must be calculated into the original cooking time. For example, let us assume that it normally takes 1½ hours to cook a given dish for immediate consumption. Also, that ½ hour is required to re-heat the majority of dishes from the frozen state. Therefore the original cooking time should not be 1½ hours but 1 hour, or the reheated dish will be overcooked. As a general rule, it takes about ½ hour to reheat the average dish, so this time must be sub-tracted from the original cooking time wherever possible. The time for reheating can be shortened if you're fortunate enough to have a micro-wave oven.

When preparing a given dish for your family, it's almost as easy to prepare enough for several additional meals. When the dish is ½ hour from completion, remove all but what is required for that evening's meal and freeze the balance in portions suitable for one meal. The recipes that follow have been designed so that you can prepare dinner for immediate use and still cook properly for the freezer.

Convenient new freezer containers are constantly appearing. Some can be used for heating and serving. Investigate the types and sizes best suited to your own needs. Too much stress cannot be placed upon proper protection of foods to be frozen. Whether the food is raw or cooked, it must be wrapped so that as much air as possible is excluded from the package. For storage longer than 1 week, it should be overwrapped in moisture-vaporproof wrap. To freeze foods quickly, cover with foil or Saran wrap and freeze. Then overwrap and return to the freezer. When thawing, keep foods wrapped unless otherwise specified.

Specific instructions are set forth for individual recipes, but the following are *basic* rules for everything:

1　Undercook foods by approximately ½ hour (the average length of time required to reheat in most cases).

2　Cool as quickly as possible by placing pot or dish in ice water, over ice, or in the refrigerator.

3　Skim as much fat as possible from the dish (may be added when reheating).

4 Wrap or pack in moistureproof containers or materials. Proper wrapping is one of the most important factors for retaining food flavor. If air touches the food, it causes freezer burn, drying the food. This applies to both cooked and uncooked food.

5 Do not overfill containers; leave about 1 inch leeway at the top to allow for expansion.

6 Label each package with the name, number of servings, and date. For example: Roast duck with cherry sauce, 4, October 8.

7 Place freshly prepared dishes in the back of the freezer and bring older ones gradually to the top and front so they will not be overlooked.

8 Don't keep foods longer than the times specified under the individual categories.

PROBLEMS THAT OCCUR IN FREEZING FOODS

In recent years great strides have been made in understanding how to handle foods to be frozen, but there are still some foods and dishes that require special care. The list below is for your general knowledge, and can be applied to all dishes to be frozen.

FOOD	PROBLEM	SOLUTION
Potatoes, cooked	Loss of texture	Do not add to stews or other cooked dishes before freezing; add when reheating.

FOOD	PROBLEM	SOLUTION
Rice, noodles, and macaroni, cooked	Loss of texture	Freeze only if in sauce or gravy, or add when reheating dish.
Creamed soups	Separate or curdle	Add milk or cream when reheating.
Creamed foods	Become rancid	Use as little fat as possible; reheat over very low heat.
Chicken dishes, cooked	Meat separates or shreds	Freeze when chicken is partially cooked.
Poultry or meat cut in small pieces, cooked	Loss of flavor	Cover with sauce or gravy before freezing.
Fatty meats, cooked	Become rancid	Cut away excess fat before freezing.
Rich sauces	Curdle, separate, or become runny	When reheating, mix almost constantly until very smooth.
Garlic	Develops off-flavor	Add when reheating.

Some foods can not be frozen, so don't attempt it. Here are a few of the absolute "don'ts."

FOOD	PROBLEM
Raw clams	Lose texture, become tough
Hard-cooked eggs	Become tough and rubbery
Milk custards	Curdle
Mayonnaise	Curdles
Salad greens	Lose crisp texture

EGG WHITES Freeze each egg white in individual-ice-cube trays, wrap, and seal; you can then use one at a time. Larger numbers can be frozen in covered containers. Label with number of egg whites. This is particularly useful when making lemon meringue pies; the egg whites will be in the freezer with the pie, ready to be whipped into a meringue. Thaw 4 hours.

EGG YOLKS Stir lightly and add 1 teaspoon salt for each cup of yolks. 1 tablespoon sugar may be added instead of the salt, but then they can only be used for sweet dishes.

WHOLE EGGS Follow instructions for yolks.

BROTH AND STOCKS Freeze in ice-cube trays, then remove and wrap, seal, label, and return to freezer. A cube added to soup or stew is a marvelous addition.

STEWS AND CASSEROLES Line a casserole with foil; freeze stew in it, then lift out. Wrap, seal, label, and return to freezer. Heat in original casserole.

HERBS Chives, dill, chervil, parsley, and tarragon can all be frozen ready for use. Wash and dry thoroughly, then chop. Pack in small freezer containers, or wrap in foil, Saran, or freezer paper. Use from the frozen state without thawing.

APPETIZERS

Unexpected guests for cocktails are no longer a problem—prepared canapés, dips, and hors d'oeuvres can be ready in a matter of minutes when the freezer is well stocked.

To prepare canapés, spread the bread with butter; do not use mayonnaise or salad dressings. Sliced meats or spreads of meat or fish are excellent for freezing, but avoid raw vegetables or hard-cooked egg mixtures. Open-faced canapés should be frozen before wrapping; place on a baking sheet or in aluminum-foil pans to freeze. Then pack in layers with freezer paper between each layer. When ready to use, thaw for 30 minutes. Pinwheel sandwiches may be frozen in rolls, then sliced and heated before serving.

BEAN APPETIZER SPREAD

2 cups dried white beans
3 teaspoons salt
3 tablespoons cider vinegar
½ teaspoon freshly ground black pepper
2 tablespoons olive oil
¼ cup finely chopped onions
3 tablespoons minced parsley

Wash the beans, cover with water, and bring to a boil. Let soak 1 hour. Drain and cover with fresh water. Bring to a boil, cover loosely, and cook over over low heat 1½ hours or until very tender. Add 1½ teaspoons salt after 45 minutes. Drain and mash the beans, or purée in an electric blender. Mix in the vinegar, pepper, and remaining salt. Cool. Pack half the mixture into a container; seal, label, and freeze.

FOR IMMEDIATE SERVICE

Add the olive oil, onions, and parsley to the remaining bean mixture. Taste for seasoning. Serve with sesame-seed crackers or toast.

TO SERVE FROM FROZEN STATE

Remove bean mixture 5 hours before serving time and let thaw, covered. Mix in 2 tablespoons olive oil, ¼ cup finely chopped onions, and 3 tablespoons minced parsley. Taste for seasoning.
Makes about 4 cups.

CHEESE BALLS

1½ cups sifted flour
¼ teaspoon salt
¾ cup butter
3 cups grated American cheese

Sift the flour and salt into a bowl; work in the butter with the fingers. Add the cheese and blend until smooth. Wrap in waxed paper and chill 1 hour. Shape into ½-inch balls. Pack the number you want to freeze in layers in freezer containers, separating the layers with 2 sheets of freezer paper.

FOR IMMEDIATE USE

Arrange on a baking sheet and bake in a preheated 350° oven 10 minutes, or until delicately browned.

TO SERVE FROM FROZEN STATE

Arrange on a cooky sheet and bake in a preheated 425° oven 12 minutes, or until browned. Serve hot or cold.

Makes about 7 dozen.

VARIATIONS

CHILI-CHEESE BALLS

Add 2 teaspoons chili powder to the flour mixture. Proceed as directed.

CHEESE-CORN-MEAL BALLS

Use ¾ cup sifted flour and ¾ cup sifted corn meal in place of the 1½ cups flour. Proceed as directed. Sprinkle the tops with sesame seed if desired.

CURRY-CHEESE BALLS

Add 2 teaspoons curry powder to the flour mixture. Proceed as directed.

CHEESE STICKS

2 cups sifted flour
1 teaspoon salt
1 teaspoon double-acting baking powder
⅜ pound (¾ cup) butter
1 egg yolk
¾ cup milk
2 cups grated Cheddar cheese

Sift the flour, salt, and baking powder into a bowl; cut in the butter with a pastry blender or 2 knives. Beat the egg yolk and milk together; mix into the flour mixture until a ball of dough is formed. Chill 1 hour. Roll out the dough ⅛ inch thick on a lightly floured surface. Sprinkle half the dough with half the cheese and fold over, sealing the edges. Fold in half again and roll out ¼ inch thick. Sprinkle with the remaining cheese and repeat folding and rolling. Roll out again ¼ inch thick and cut into strips ½ × 3 inches. Arrange the number you want to freeze in a container, with aluminum foil between the layers. Seal, label, and freeze.

FOR IMMEDIATE SERVICE
Arrange on a baking sheet; bake in a preheated 450° oven 10 minutes, or until delicately browned. Serve hot or cold.

TO SERVE FROM FROZEN STATE
Carefully remove the sticks from the containers. Arrange on a baking sheet; bake in a preheated 450° oven 12 minutes, or until delicately browned. Serve hot or cold.
Makes about 60.

CRAB-MEAT FRITTERS

3 tablespoons butter
2 tablespoons minced onions
3 tablespoons flour
1 teaspoon salt
1 cup light cream
¾ pound flaked crab meat
1 tablespoon minced parsley
Fat for deep frying

Melt the butter in a saucepan; sauté the onions 5 minutes. Blend in the flour and salt, then gradually add the cream, stirring steadily to the boiling point. Cook over low heat 5 minutes. Cool 5 minutes and mix in the crab meat and parsley. Cool 15 minutes. Shape the mixture into walnut-sized balls. Pack the number you want to freeze in containers, with double layers of foil or freezer paper between the layers. Wrap, seal, label, and freeze.

FOR IMMEDIATE SERVICE
Heat the fat (about 5 inches deep) to 390°. Drop the balls into it and fry until browned on all sides. Drain, pierce with cocktail picks, and serve hot.

TO SERVE FROM FROZEN STATE
Heat fat (about 5 inches deep) to 375°. Drop the frozen balls into it and fry until browned on all sides. Drain and pierce with cocktail picks. Serve hot.
Makes about 48 balls.

FISH BALLS

3 tablespoons butter
¾ cup diced onions
1 clove garlic, minced
½ cup dried flaked coconut
1½ pounds fish fillets (sole, halibut, snapper)
1 egg
1 teaspoon salt
¼ teaspoon pepper
2 teaspoons curry powder
½ cup fine dry bread crumbs
Fat for frying

Melt 2 tablespoons butter in a skillet; sauté the onions and garlic 10 minutes. Remove from skillet. Melt remaining butter and sauté coconut, stirring constantly, until delicately browned. Watch carefully to avoid burning. Grind the fish, onions, garlic, and coconut in a food chopper, or chop until smooth. Blend in the egg, salt, pepper, and curry powder. Shape into ½-inch balls and roll in the bread crumbs. Freeze the number you want on a baking sheet, then pack in freezer containers with freezer paper between the layers. Seal, label, and freeze. Pack by the dozen.

FOR IMMEDIATE SERVICE
Sauté the balls in 1 inch of hot fat until browned on all sides. Drain and serve speared with cocktail picks.

TO SERVE FROM FROZEN STATE
Brown the frozen balls in 1½ inches of hot fat. Drain and serve hot.
Makes about 60.

CHINESE LOBSTER ROLL

2 eggs
½ teaspoon salt
1 cup water
1 cup sifted flour
¾ cup peanut or salad oil
¼ cup grated carrots
¼ cup minced onions
¼ cup chopped water chestnuts
1 cup diced cooked or canned lobster
¼ cup chopped walnuts
½ teaspoon salt
¼ teaspoon freshly ground black pepper

Beat the eggs, salt, and water together. Stir in the flour until smooth. Heat 1 teaspoon oil in a 7-inch skillet; pour in enough of the batter (about 2 tablespoons) to coat the bottom lightly. Tip pan to spread batter evenly. Cook over low heat until bottom browns. Turn out onto a napkin, browned side down. Prepare the remaining batter, adding oil as needed. Reserve 2 tablespoons batter to seal the rolls.

Heat 2 tablespoons oil in a skillet; sauté the carrots and onions 5 minutes. Combine with the water chestnuts, lobster, walnuts, salt, and pepper. Place 2 tablespoons of the mixture on each pancake (unbrowned side) and tuck in opposite ends, then roll up. Seal with a little of the reserved batter. Chill. Pack 5 rolls into a container; seal, label, and freeze.

FOR IMMEDIATE SERVICE

Heat the remaining oil in a skillet; fry the remaining rolls in it until browned and crisp on both sides. Drain, cut in half, and serve hot. Chinese *duk* sauce and mustard should be served with the rolls.

TO SERVE FROM FROZEN STATE

Heat ½ cup peanut or salad oil in a skillet; fry the frozen rolls in it until browned on both sides. Drain and serve as above.

Makes 10 rolls.

HAM AND CHICKEN BALLS

¼ pound boiled ham
1½ cups diced cooked chicken
1 slice bread
2 pimentos
⅛ teaspoon dried ground chili peppers
½ teaspoon salt
2 eggs
¾ cup dry bread crumbs
½ cup salad oil

Grind together the ham, chicken, bread, and pimentos. Blend in the chili peppers, salt, and eggs. Shape into walnut-sized balls; roll in the bread crumbs. Arrange the number you want to freeze on a cooky sheet and freeze. Remove from sheet and pack into containers; seal, label, and freeze.

FOR IMMEDIATE SERVICE

Heat the oil in a skillet; brown the balls on all sides. Drain and spear with cocktail picks. Serve hot.

TO SERVE FROM FROZEN STATE

Heat ½ cup salad oil in a skillet; fry the frozen balls in it until browned and hot.

Makes 65–70.

HORS D'OEUVRE ROLLS

2 cups sifted flour
½ teaspoon salt
1 cup butter
4 tablespoons sour cream

Sift the flour and salt into a bowl; work in the butter with the fingers. Add the sour cream and mix until smooth. Form into a ball, wrap in waxed paper, and chill 2 hours or overnight.

Divide the dough in 6 pieces and roll out ⅛ inch thick. Spread with the desired filling and roll up like a jelly roll. Wrap the number you want to freeze in foil; seal, label, and freeze.

FOR IMMEDIATE SERVICE

Place the rolls on a baking sheet. Bake in a preheated 400° oven 15 minutes or until browned. Cut in ½-inch slices.

TO SERVE FROM FROZEN STATE

Unwrap and place on a baking sheet. With a sharp knife make indentations ½ inch apart. Bake in a preheated 425° oven 15 minutes or until browned. Cut through and serve hot.

Each roll makes about 16.

MUSHROOM FILLING

3 tablespoons butter
½ cup diced onions
1 pound mushrooms, chopped
1 teaspoon salt
¼ teaspoon freshly ground black pepper
2 hard-cooked egg yolks, chopped
2 tablespoons sour cream
2 tablespoons dry bread crumbs

Melt the butter in a skillet; sauté the onions 10 minutes. Add the mushrooms and cook over medium heat 5 minutes, stirring occasionally. If any liquid remains, turn up the heat and cook until it evaporates. Cool.

Blend in the salt, pepper, egg yolks, sour cream, and bread crumbs. Taste for seasoning. Spread on the dough and proceed as directed.

LIVER FILLING
    3 tablespoons butter or rendered chicken fat
    ½ cup chopped onions
    ¾ pound chicken livers or calves' liver, cubed
    1½ teaspoons salt
    ½ teaspoon freshly ground black pepper

Melt 1 tablespoon fat in a skillet; sauté the onions 10 minutes. Remove from skillet. Melt remaining fat in the skillet; sauté the liver 5 minutes or until no pink remains. Grind the onions and liver in a food chopper or chop until very smooth. Season with salt and pepper. Taste for seasoning and cool. Spread on the dough and proceed as directed.

CHEESE FILLING
    8 ounces cream cheese
    6 anchovy fillets, drained and chopped
    2 tablespoons chopped capers
    ¼ cup chopped green olives
    ½ teaspoon Worcestershire sauce

Blend all ingredients and spread on the dough. Proceed as directed.

TUNA PINWHEELS

    1 3-ounce package cream cheese
    1 can (7¾ ounces) tuna fish, drained and flaked
    ½ teaspoon freshly ground black pepper
    ½ teaspoon chili powder
  16 thin slices fresh white bread
    4 tablespoons soft butter

Cream the cheese and blend in the tuna fish, pepper, and chili powder.

Trim the crusts from the bread. Roll lightly with a rolling pin on a slightly dampened towel. Spread each slice with some butter and then about 1 tablespoon of the mixture and roll up like a jelly roll. Wrap in aluminum foil and chill. Overwrap and label the ones you want to freeze.

FOR IMMEDIATE SERVICE

Slice the rolls ½ inch thick. Arrange on a buttered baking sheet; place under the broiler until browned on both sides.

TO SERVE FROM FROZEN STATE

Unwrap and slice ½ inch thick. Arrange on a buttered baking sheet. Bake in a preheated 450° oven 10 minutes.

Each roll makes about 5 slices.

SARDINE PINWHEELS

Substitute ½ cup mashed skinless and boneless sardines for the tuna fish. Omit the chili powder and add 1 teaspoon prepared mustard. Proceed as directed above.

TURKEY OR CHICKEN TURNOVERS

3 cups chopped cooked turkey or chicken
2 tablespoons minced parsley
½ cup chopped onions, sautéed
6 tablespoons sour cream
1½ teaspoons salt
¼ teaspoon freshly ground black pepper
Pastry for 2-crust pie

Mix together the poultry, parsley, onions, sour cream, salt, and pepper. Roll out the pastry ⅛ inch thick and cut in 3-inch circles. Place a tablespoon of the filling on each and fold the dough over it, sealing the edges well. Pack the number you want to freeze with double layers of foil or freezer paper between the layers. Wrap, seal, label, and freeze.

FOR IMMEDIATE SERVICE

Arrange the turnovers on a baking sheet. Bake in a preheated 375° oven 12 minutes or until browned.

TO SERVE FROM FROZEN STATE

Arrange the frozen turnovers on a baking sheet. Bake in a preheated 400° oven 15 minutes, or until browned.

Makes about 36.

BEEF TURNOVERS

Substitute 3 cups sautéed ground beef for the chicken or turkey, and add 3 mashed hard-cooked egg yolks. Proceed as directed.

COCKTAIL BISCUITS

3 tablespoons butter
3 cups biscuit mix
4 tablespoons minced scallions (green onions)
3 tablespoons minced pimentos
1 teaspoon chili powder
1 cup light cream

Preheat the oven to 450°.

Cut the butter into the biscuit mix. Stir in the scallions, pimentos, and chili powder, then the cream. Knead lightly; roll out ¼ inch thick on a lightly floured surface. Cut into ¾- to 1-inch rounds with a cooky or biscuit cutter. Arrange on a cooky sheet. Bake 8 minutes; remove the number you want to freeze and cool. Pack into containers; seal, label, and freeze.

FOR IMMEDIATE SERVICE

Bake remaining biscuits 2 minutes longer, or until delicately browned. Serve hot, as they are, or split and spread with grated cheese or butter.

TO SERVE FROM FROZEN STATE

Arrange frozen biscuits on a cooky sheet and bake in a preheated 375° oven 7 minutes, or until hot. Follow above serving instructions.

Makes about 4 dozen.

QUICHE LORRAINE

Pastry for 2 9-inch pie shells
1 pound (4 cups) Swiss cheese, grated
2 tablespoons flour
8 egg yolks
2 cups light cream
1 teaspoon salt
¼ teaspoon nutmeg

Preheat the oven to 375°.

Line 2 9-inch pie plates with the pastry. Toss the cheese and flour together and fill the shells with it. Beat the egg yolks, cream, salt, and nutmeg together and pour over the cheese. Bake 25 minutes and remove 1 pie. Cool on a cake rack; wrap, seal, label, and freeze.

FOR IMMEDIATE SERVICE

Continue baking the remaining pie 10 minutes, or until browned and set. Cut in wedges and serve.

TO SERVE FROM FROZEN STATE

Unwrap frozen pie and bake in a preheated 325° oven 25 minutes, or until hot and browned.

CURRIED PASTRY HORS D'OEUVRES

2 cups plus 2 tablespoons sifted flour
1½ teaspoons salt
½ pound butter
6 tablespoons sour cream
1 cup milk
1½ tablespoons curry powder
2 cups chopped cooked chicken, beef, or veal

Sift 2 cups flour and ¾ teaspoon salt into a bowl. Work in the butter (reserving 2 tablespoons) with the fingers. Add the sour cream, mixing until a dough is formed. Wrap in waxed paper and chill 2 hours or overnight.

Melt the remaining butter; stir in the remaining flour. Gradually add the milk, stirring constantly to the boiling point. Add the curry powder and remaining salt. Cook over low heat 5 minutes, stirring occasionally. Stir in the meat. Cool.

Roll out the dough ⅛ inch thick on a lightly floured surface. Cut into 3-inch circles. Place a teaspoon of the meat mixture on each. Fold over the dough, sealing the edges with water or egg. Pack the number you want to freeze in freezer cartons, 12 to a carton. If packed in layers, separate with 2 sheets of freezer paper. Wrap, seal, label, and freeze.

FOR IMMEDIATE SERVICE

Arrange on a baking sheet. Bake in a preheated 375° oven 12 minutes, or until browned.

TO SERVE FROM FROZEN STATE

Arrange frozen pastries on a baking sheet. Bake in a preheated 400° oven 15 minutes, or until browned.

Makes about 72.

SOUPS

Almost all soups freeze beautifully, with one or two exceptions—if the soup contains potatoes, they should be added when reheating, and so should milk or cream. Pack the soup in freezer containers or jars, allowing 1 inch headroom. When ready to reheat, hold the container under hot running water to loosen, and turn into a saucepan. Cook over very low heat until hot, stirring frequently.

You can also freeze concentrated stock. Cook the skimmed and strained broth until reduced to half its original quantity, then freeze in ice-cube trays. Wrap individual cubes and return to freezer. Add to stews, or heat with an equal amount of water to serve as soup.

CREAM OF CORN SOUP

6 cups fresh, frozen, or canned corn kernels
4 tablespoons butter
1 cup chopped onions
5 tablespoons flour
2 cups fresh or canned chicken broth
2 cups milk
1 cup light cream
Salt
⅛ teaspoon white pepper
⅛ teaspoon paprika

Grind the corn in a food chopper. Melt the butter in a sauce-pan; sauté the onions until tender, but do not let brown. Stir in the flour, then gradually add the broth, mixing steadily to the boiling point. Add the corn; cook over low heat 10 minutes. Pour off half the mixture and cool. Turn into a container; seal, label, and freeze.

FOR TONIGHT'S DINNER
To the remaining corn mixture, add the milk, cream, and salt and pepper to taste. Heat to the boiling point and serve in cups, sprinkled with paprika.

TO SERVE FROM FROZEN STATE
Turn into a double boiler and cook, covered, over hot water until thawed. Place over direct heat and mix in 2 cups milk, 1 cup light cream, ⅛ teaspoon white pepper, and salt to taste. Heat to the boiling point and serve in cups, with a sprinkling of paprika.
Serves 6–7 each time.

TOMATO SOUP

8 pounds very ripe tomatoes, diced
1 cup water
2 onions, diced
2 teaspoons salt
¼ cup lemon juice
¼ cup sugar
2 tablespoons butter
1 tablespoon flour
¾ cup milk

Combine the tomatoes, water, onions, and salt in a saucepan. Bring to a boil. Cover and cook over low heat 30 minutes. Stir in the lemon juice and sugar; cook 5 minutes. Purée the mixture in an electric blender, then strain; or force through a food mill. Pour two thirds of the soup into a bowl and cool, then pour into 2 containers. Seal, label, and freeze.

FOR TONIGHT'S DINNER
Melt the butter; blend in the flour. Gradually add the milk, stirring steadily to the boiling point. Mix into the remaining soup. Heat and taste for seasoning.

TO SERVE FROM FROZEN STATE
Turn contents of one container into a saucepan, cover, and cook over low heat until thawed. Mix in white sauce as prepared above. Heat and taste for seasoning.
Serves 6–8 each time.

GREEN PEA SOUP

3 tablespoons butter
1½ cups sliced onions
3 cups shredded lettuce
4 tablespoons minced parsley
4 packages frozen green peas
4 cups fresh or canned chicken broth
2 quarts water
2 teaspoons salt
¼ teaspoon white pepper
½ cup heavy cream

Melt the butter in a saucepan; sauté the onions, lettuce, and parsley for 10 minutes. Add the peas, broth, water, salt, and pepper. Cover and cook over low heat 45 minutes. Purée in an electric blender or force through a food mill. Cool two thirds of the soup; pour into 2 containers. Seal, label, and freeze.

FOR TONIGHT'S DINNER
Stir the cream into the remaining soup; heat and taste for seasoning.

TO SERVE FROM FROZEN STATE
Turn contents of one container into a saucepan, cover, and cook over low heat until thawed. Stir in ½ cup heavy cream. Heat and taste for seasoning.
Serves 6–8 each time.

CREAM OF PEA AND NOODLE SOUP

4 cups split peas
3 quarts water
Ham bone
6 cloves
3 onions
2 carrots, sliced
2 leeks, sliced
3 tablespoons butter
½ cup finely chopped spinach
½ cup shredded ham
½ cup cooked fine noodles
1½ teaspoons salt
1 teaspoon sugar
¼ teaspoon white pepper
½ cup heavy cream

Use the quick-cooking split peas. Wash thoroughly and combine in a saucepan with the water, ham bone, the cloves stuck in the onions, the carrots, and leeks. Bring to a boil, cover, and cook over low heat 1½ hours, or until peas are tender. Discard bone and onions. Purée the mixture in an electric blender or force through a food mill. Transfer two thirds of the mixture to a bowl and cool quickly. Pour into 2 containers; seal, label, and freeze.

FOR TONIGHT'S DINNER

Melt 1 tablespoon butter in a saucepan; sauté the spinach 3 minutes. Add the remaining soup, ham, noodles, salt, sugar, pepper, cream, and remaining butter. Heat, taste for seasoning, and serve.

TO SERVE FROM FROZEN STATE

Turn contents of one container into the top of a double boiler; place over hot water, cover, and cook until thawed. Sauté ½ cup chopped spinach in 1 tablespoon butter. Add to the soup with ½ cup shredded ham, ½ cup cooked fine noodles, 1½ teaspoons salt,

1 teaspoon sugar, ¼ teaspoon white pepper, ½ cup heavy cream, and 2 tablespoons butter. Cook over direct low heat until very hot. Taste for seasoning.

Serves 4–6 each time.

FRENCH ONION SOUP

4 tablespoons butter
6 cups thinly sliced onions
1 tablespoon flour
3 quarts fresh or canned beef broth
½ teaspoon freshly ground black pepper
Salt
French bread
Grated Gruyère or Swiss cheese

Melt the butter in a saucepan; sauté the onions until soft and golden. Stir in the flour. Add the broth gradually, stirring steadily; cook over low heat 20 minutes. Season with the pepper, and salt to taste. Pour half the soup into a container; cool, seal, label, and freeze.

FOR TONIGHT'S DINNER
Divide the remaining soup among 6 ovenproof bowls or casseroles. Place a slice of bread in each and sprinkle heavily with the cheese. Place in a 450° oven for 5 minutes, or until the cheese is lightly browned and melted.

TO SERVE FROM FROZEN STATE
Turn into a saucepan; cook over low heat until hot. Divide among 6 ovenproof bowls or casseroles. Place a slice of French bread in each and sprinkle heavily with grated Gruyère or Swiss cheese. Place in a 450° oven for 5 minutes, or until cheese is lightly browned and melted.

Serves 6 each time.

CREAM OF SPINACH SOUP

3 pounds spinach or 3 packages frozen
3 tablespoons butter
4 tablespoons grated onions
4 tablespoons flour
6 cups chicken broth
¼ teaspoon white pepper
¼ teaspoon nutmeg
2 egg yolks
1½ cups light cream

If fresh spinach is used, wash thoroughly and chop. Thaw frozen spinach.

Melt the butter in a saucepan; sauté the onions 5 minutes. Add the spinach; cook over low heat 5 minutes, stirring frequently. Blend in the flour, then the broth, pepper, and nutmeg. Bring to a boil and cook over low heat 15 minutes. Purée in a blender or force through a sieve. Cool half the soup; pour into a container. Seal, label, and freeze.

FOR TONIGHT'S DINNER

Beat the egg yolks and cream together; gradually add the remaining hot soup, stirring steadily to prevent curdling. Heat, but do not let boil. Taste for seasoning.

TO SERVE FROM FROZEN STATE

Turn into a saucepan; cover and cook over low heat until thawed and hot. Beat 2 egg yolks with 1½ cups light cream. Gradually add the hot spinach mixture, stirring steadily to prevent curdling. Heat, but do not let boil.

Serves 4–6 each time.

LENTIL SOUP

2 cups lentils
3 tablespoons butter
1 cup chopped onions
2 quarts water
2 cups canned tomatoes
2 carrots, grated
1 tablespoon salt
¼ teaspoon freshly ground black pepper
⅛ teaspoon thyme
1 bay leaf
½ cup heavy cream

Wash the lentils and drain. Melt the butter in a saucepan; sauté the onions 10 minutes. Add the water, tomatoes, carrots, salt, pepper, thyme, bay leaf, and lentils. Bring to a boil, cover, and cook over low heat 45 minutes. Discard the bay leaf. Cool half the soup; pour into a container. Seal, label, and freeze.

FOR TONIGHT'S DINNER

Add ½ cup heavy cream to the remaining soup. Heat and taste for seasoning.

TO SERVE FROM FROZEN STATE

Turn into a saucepan, cover, and cook over low heat until thawed. Stir in ½ cup heavy cream. Heat and taste for seasoning.

Serves 6–8 each time. Freeze in smaller quantities if you don't need this much.

MINESTRONE

2 cups dried red beans
2 beef bones
8 quarts water
3 tablespoons olive or salad oil
1 cup minced onions
1 pound ground beef
3 cups shredded cabbage
2 cups diced carrots
2 (20-ounce) cans tomatoes
1 cup diced celery
1 tablespoon salt
½ teaspoon pepper
½ teaspoon oregano
1 clove garlic, minced
1 cup peas, fresh or frozen
1 cup green beans, fresh or frozen
1 cup elbow macaroni
Grated Parmesan cheese

Wash the beans thoroughly. Bring to a boil and let soak 1 hour. Drain.

Combine the beans, bones, and water in a large kettle. Bring to a boil, cover, and cook over medium heat 2 hours.

Heat the oil in a skillet; sauté the onions and beef until browned. Add to the soup with the cabbage, carrots, tomatoes, celery, salt, pepper, and oregano. Cover and cook over low heat 30 minutes. Remove two thirds of the mixture and chill. Pack in 2 jars or freezer containers.

FOR TONIGHT'S DINNER

To the remaining soup, add the garlic, peas, green beans, and macaroni. Cook 15 minutes. Taste for seasoning and serve with the cheese.

TO SERVE FROM FROZEN STATE

Turn contents of one container into a saucepan. Cover and cook over low heat until it begins to thaw. Add 1 minced clove garlic, 1 cup peas, 1 cup green beans, and 1 cup elbow macaroni. Cover and cook over low heat 20 minutes, or until vegetables and macaroni are tender and soup very hot.

Serves 6–8 each time.

GOULASH SOUP

3 pounds beef (cross rib, chuck, etc.)
6 tablespoons butter
3 cups diced onions
2 tablespoons paprika
2½ teaspoons salt
½ teaspoon pepper
2½ quarts water
2 8-ounce cans tomato sauce
½ cup sour cream

Cut the meat in 1-inch cubes. Melt half the butter in a Dutch oven or heavy saucepan. Sauté the onions over low heat for 15 minutes, stirring frequently. Remove and set aside. Melt remaining butter in the saucepan; brown the meat on all sides. Return the onions to the saucepan and sprinkle with the paprika, salt, and pepper. Add the water and tomato sauce, cover, and cook over low heat 2 hours. Transfer half the soup to a bowl; place in cold water to chill. Pack in a freezer container; seal, label, and freeze.

FOR TONIGHT'S DINNER

Continue cooking the remaining soup 30 minutes. Taste for seasoning and stir in the sour cream. Heat, but do not let boil.

TO SERVE FROM FROZEN STATE

Turn into a saucepan. Cover and cook over low heat 30 minutes or until very hot. Taste for seasoning and stir in ½ cup sour cream.

Serves 6–8 each time.

VEGETABLE CHOWDER

3 tablespoons butter
1 cup chopped onions
1 pound mushrooms, sliced
2 cups diced carrots
6 cups chicken broth
1 bay leaf
½ teaspoon thyme
½ teaspoon nutmeg
½ teaspoon white pepper
3 cups shelled lima beans
1 cup diced potatoes
1½ cups light cream

Melt the butter in a saucepan; sauté the onions 5 minutes. Stir in the mushrooms and carrots; sauté 3 minutes. Add the broth, bay leaf, thyme, nutmeg, and pepper. Bring to a boil and add the lima beans. Cover and cook over low heat 15 minutes. Transfer half the soup to a bowl or saucepan; place in cold water or over ice to cool quickly. Pour into a container; seal, label, and freeze.

FOR TONIGHT'S DINNER

Add the potatoes to the remaining soup; cook over low heat 15 minutes, or until potatoes are tender. Mix in the cream; heat and taste for seasoning.

TO SERVE FROM FROZEN STATE

Turn into a saucepan, cover, and cook over low heat until thawed. Add 1 cup diced cooked potatoes and 1½ cups light cream. Heat and taste for seasoning.

Serves 4–6 each time.

RUMANIAN ONION SOUP

4 tablespoons butter
6 cups chopped onions
8 cups fresh or canned beef broth
2 cups dry white wine
1½ tablespoons cider vinegar
1½ tablespoons sugar
2 teaspoons salt
½ teaspoon white pepper
¾ cup heavy cream
1 tablespoon minced parsley

Melt the butter in a saucepan; sauté the onions until browned. Add the broth, cover, and cook over low heat 45 minutes. Purée in an electric blender or force through a sieve. Stir in the wine, vinegar, sugar, salt, and pepper. Bring to a boil and cook over low heat 10 minutes. Cool half the soup; pour into a container. Seal, label, and freeze.

FOR TONIGHT'S DINNER

Add the cream and parsley to the remaining soup. Taste for seasoning; heat but do not let boil.

TO SERVE FROM FROZEN STATE

Turn into a saucepan; cook over low heat until thawed. Stir in ¾ cup heavy cream and 1 tablespoon minced parsley. Taste for seasoning; heat but do not let boil.

Serves 6–8 each time.

CHICKEN GUMBO

1 5-pound fowl, disjointed
4 quarts water
1 tablespoon salt
2 stalks celery
2 sprigs parsley
6 tablespoons butter
½ cup chopped onions
2½ cups peeled and diced tomatoes
1 pound okra, cut in ¼-inch slices
1 teaspoon Worcestershire sauce
½ cup cooked rice
2 slices crisp bacon, crumbled
½ teaspoon freshly ground black pepper

Wash the chicken and combine with the water, salt, celery, and parsley in a large kettle. Bring to a boil, cover, and cook over low heat 1½ hours, or until chicken is tender. Remove the chicken and cube the meat. Strain the broth.

Melt the butter in a saucepan; sauté the onions 10 minutes. Mix in the chicken until browned. Add the broth, tomatoes, and okra; cover and cook over low heat 15 minutes. Transfer half the soup to a bowl; place in cold water or over ice to cool quickly. Skim the fat. Pour into a container; seal, label, and freeze.

FOR TONIGHT'S DINNER
Continue cooking the soup 10 minutes longer. Stir in the Worcestershire sauce, rice, bacon, and pepper. Taste for seasoning.

TO SERVE FROM FROZEN STATE
Turn into a saucepan, cover, and cook over low heat until thawed. Add 1 teaspoon Worcestershire sauce, ½ cup cooked rice, 2 slices crumbled crisp bacon, and ½ teaspoon freshly ground black pepper. Bring to a boil and taste for seasoning.

Serves 6–8 each time.

NEW ORLEANS GUMBO

4 tablespoons butter
1 pound stewing beef, cut in 1-inch cubes
Beef bones
4 quarts water
1 onion
3 stalks celery
4 sprigs parsley
1 tablespoon salt
½ teaspoon freshly ground black pepper
1 cup chopped onions
2 cups fresh or frozen sliced okra
2 tablespoons sugar
4 cups canned tomatoes
½ pound crab meat

Melt 2 tablespoons butter in a large kettle; brown the meat and bones in it. Add the water, onion, celery, parsley, salt, and pepper. Bring to a boil, cover, and cook over low heat 2½ hours. Remove the meat and discard the bones. Strain the soup and skim the fat.

Melt the remaining butter in the saucepan; sauté the chopped onions and okra in it 5 minutes. Add the sugar, tomatoes, and soup. Cover and cook over low heat 45 minutes. Cool two thirds of the soup and pour into 2 containers. Seal, label, and freeze.

FOR TONIGHT'S DINNER

Add the crab meat to the remaining soup and cook over low heat 15 minutes. Taste for seasoning. Serve with 2 tablespoons of cooked rice in each bowl.

TO SERVE FROM FROZEN STATE

Turn contents of one container into a saucepan; cover and cook over low heat until thawed. Add ½ pound crab meat; re-cover and cook 15 minutes, or until very hot. Taste for seasoning. Serve with 2 tablespoons cooked rice in each bowl.

Serves 4–6 each time.

CHICK PEA SOUP

3 cups chick peas
2 pounds stewing beef
1 beef bone
4 quarts water
1 tablespoon butter
1 cup diced onions
1 tablespoon salt
2 teaspoons paprika
1½ cups cubed potatoes
2 Spanish or Italian sausages

Wash the chick peas, cover with water, and bring to a boil; let soak 1 hour. Drain.

Cut the meat in 1-inch cubes and combine with the bone, water, and chick peas. Bring to a boil, cover, and cook over low heat 1 hour. Melt the butter in a skillet; sauté the onions 5 minutes. Add to the soup with salt and paprika. Cook over low heat 30 minutes. Discard bone. Transfer half the soup to a bowl or saucepan; place in cold water or over ice to cool quickly. Skim the fat. Pour into a container; seal, label, and freeze.

FOR TONIGHT'S DINNER

Add the potatoes to the remaining soup. Cook 20 minutes. Slice the sausage and brown. Drain and add to the soup. Taste for seasoning.

TO SERVE FROM FROZEN STATE

Turn into a saucepan, cover, and cook over low heat until thawed. Add 1½ cups cubed potatoes; cook 20 minutes. Brown 2 sliced Spanish or Italian sausages and add. Taste for seasoning.

Serves 6–8 each time.

MEAT BALL SOUP

3 cups lentils
4 quarts water
1 29-ounce can tomatoes
4 teaspoons salt
¾ teaspoon pepper
4 tablespoons butter
1 cup diced onions
2 bay leaves
3 tablespoons chopped parsley
1 pound ground beef
1 egg, beaten
3 tablespoons flour

Wash the lentils and combine with the water, tomatoes, 2½ teaspoons salt, ½ teaspoon pepper, 3 tablespoons butter, onions, bay leaves, and parsley. Bring to a boil, cover and cook over low heat 2 hours. Discard bay leaves and purée in an electric blender or force through a food mill. Return to saucepan and cook over low heat while preparing the meat balls.

Mix the beef with the egg and remaining salt and pepper. Form into ½-inch balls and roll in the flour. Melt the remaining butter in a skillet and brown the meat balls in it. Add to the soup. Cook for 20 minutes. Chill half the soup and meat balls and then pack into jars or freezer containers, allowing 1 inch headroom. Seal, label, and freeze.

FOR IMMEDIATE SERVICE
Cook remaining soup 10 minutes longer. Taste for seasoning.

TO SERVE FROM FROZEN STATE
Turn into a saucepan, cover, and cook over very low heat until very hot, about 30 minutes. Taste for seasoning.
Serves 8 each time.

VICHYSSOISE

3 tablespoons butter
4 cups sliced leeks (white part)
1½ cups sliced onions
10 cups fresh or canned chicken broth
3 cups diced potatoes
2 stalks celery
4 sprigs parsley
Salt
2 teaspoons Worcestershire sauce
½ teaspoon white pepper
1½ cups light cream
Minced chives

Melt the butter in a saucepan; cook the leeks and onions in it over low heat (without browning) for 10 minutes. Add the broth, potatoes, celery, and parsley. Cover and cook over low heat 30 minutes. Discard the celery and parsley. Purée the soup in an electric blender or force through a sieve. Add salt to taste (depending on the amount in the broth), the Worcestershire sauce, and pepper. Cool. Pour half the soup into a freezer container; seal, label, and freeze.

FOR TONIGHT'S DINNER
Stir the cream into the remaining soup and chill. Taste for seasoning. Serve in chilled cups, sprinkled with the chives.

TO SERVE FROM FROZEN STATE
Remove container from freezer the night before you want to use the soup, and place in refrigerator. Or place container in hot water until partially thawed, then turn into a bowl until thawed. If soup is lumpy, mix in an electric blender for a few seconds, or beat with a rotary beater. Stir in 1½ cups light cream and serve in chilled cups, sprinkled with minced chives.
Serves 6–7 each time.

MANHATTAN CLAM CHOWDER

2 quarts shucked clams or 4 cans minced clams
1 strip salt pork, diced
1½ cups chopped onions
4 tablespoons flour
4 cups drained canned tomatoes
½ teaspoon freshly ground black pepper
½ teaspoon thyme
1½ cups diced potatoes

If fresh clams are used, chop them, reserving all the liquid. Measure the liquid and add water to make 3 quarts. If canned clams are used, drain and measure liquid. Add water to make 3 quarts. Sauté the salt pork and onions until browned. Stir in the flour. Add the tomatoes, pepper, thyme, and clam liquid. Bring to a boil and cook over low heat 20 minutes. Transfer two thirds of the soup to a bowl and add two thirds of the clams. Cool and pour into 2 containers. Seal, label, and freeze.

FOR TONIGHT'S DINNER
Add the potatoes to the remaining soup. Cook 15 minutes, stir in the remaining clams, and cook 3 minutes. Taste for seasoning.

TO SERVE FROM FROZEN STATE
Turn contents of one container into a saucepan; cover and cook over low heat until thawed. Add 1½ cups half-cooked diced potatoes. Continue cooking until very hot. Taste for seasoning.
Serves 4–6 each time.

ITALIAN FISH CHOWDER

4 pounds mixed white-meat fish (sea bass, whitefish, sole, etc.)
½ cup olive oil
1 cup chopped onions
1 cup grated carrots
1 cup chopped celery
½ cup minced parsley
2 cups dry white wine
1 bay leaf
2 cups canned Italian-style tomatoes
4 cups water
2 teaspoons salt
½ teaspoon freshly ground black pepper
½ teaspoon oregano

Remove the skin and bones of the fish and cut in bite-sized pieces.

Heat the oil in a saucepan; sauté the onions, carrots, celery, and parsley 10 minutes. Mix in the wine and bay leaf; cook over low heat 10 minutes. Add the fish, tomatoes, water, salt, pepper, and oregano. Bring to a boil and cook over low heat 15 minutes. Transfer half the mixture to a bowl; place in cold water or over ice to cool quickly. Pack into a container; seal, label, and freeze.

FOR TONIGHT'S DINNER

Continue cooking the chowder 15 minutes longer. Taste for seasoning, and serve with garlic-rubbed, toasted Italian or French bread.

TO SERVE FROM FROZEN STATE

Turn into a saucepan, cover, and cook over low heat 15 minutes. Remove cover and cook 15 minutes longer, or until very hot. Taste for seasoning.

Note: This is a very thick chowder, really more like a stew.

Serves 6–8 each time.

SHRIMP BISQUE

3 pounds raw shrimp, shelled and deveined
4 tablespoons butter
¼ pound mushrooms, chopped
3 tablespoons grated carrots
8 cups chicken broth
2 cups dry white wine
⅛ teaspoon nutmeg
¼ teaspoon white pepper
Dash cayenne pepper
1 cup light cream

Chop the shrimp very fine. Melt the butter in a saucepan; sauté the shrimp, mushrooms, and carrots 3 minutes. Stir in the broth, wine, nutmeg, pepper, and cayenne pepper. Bring to a boil and cook over low heat 20 minutes. Force through a sieve, rubbing through as much of the shrimp as possible. Cool half the soup and pour into a container. Seal, label, and freeze.

FOR TONIGHT'S DINNER

Add 1 cup light cream to the remaining soup. Heat and taste for seasoning.

TO SERVE FROM FROZEN STATE

Turn into a saucepan and add 1 cup light cream. Cover and cook over low heat until thawed, stirring frequently. Uncover and bring to the boiling point. Taste for seasoning.

Serves 4–6 each time.

FISH AND SEAFOOD

Fish and seafood in sauces freeze marvelously, and save a great deal of time and effort. Fried, sautéed, and broiled fish dishes are prepared quickly, so don't freeze them, as the reheating time is almost as long as the initial cooking time.

STUFFED CRABS

2 cups soft bread crumbs
1 cup water
6 tablespoons butter
1 cup chopped onions
1 cup finely chopped celery
2 tablespoons minced parsley
2 pounds crab meat
2 eggs, beaten
1¼ teaspoons salt
¼ teaspoon white pepper
½ teaspoon thyme
½ teaspoon marjoram

Soak the bread crumbs in the water. Squeeze dry. Melt the butter in a skillet; sauté the onions and celery 10 minutes, stirring frequently. Mix together the sautéed mixture, the parsley, crab meat, eggs, salt, pepper, thyme, marjoram, and bread. Divide the mixture among 12 crab shells or ramekins. Place 6 on a pan and freeze. When frozen, wrap, seal, label, and return to freezer.

FOR TONIGHT'S DINNER
Dot the remaining shells with a little butter. Bake in a 450° oven 15 minutes, or until browned.

TO SERVE FROM FROZEN STATE
Unwrap the shells and place on a baking sheet. Dot with a little butter. Bake in a 400° oven 25 minutes, or until browned and hot.
Serves 6 each time.

COQUILLES SAINT-JACQUES

  3 pounds scallops
  3 cups dry white wine
  1 onion
  1 bay leaf
  2 stalks celery
  2 teaspoons salt
  ½ teaspoon white pepper
  6 tablespoons butter
  ¾ pound mushrooms, chopped
  ½ cup chopped onions
  1 tablespoon minced parsley
  5 tablespoons flour
  3 egg yolks
  6 tablespoons heavy cream
  2 tablespoons bread crumbs

Wash the scallops, drain, and slice. Combine in a saucepan the wine, onion, bay leaf, celery, salt, and pepper. Bring to a boil and add the scallops; cook over low heat 5 minutes. Drain, reserving the strained stock.

Melt 2 tablespoons butter in a skillet; sauté the mushrooms, onions, and parsley 10 minutes, stirring frequently.

Melt the remaining butter in a saucepan; blend in the flour. Gradually add the stock, stirring steadily to the boiling point. Cook over low heat 5 minutes. Beat the egg yolks and cream together; gradually add the hot sauce, stirring steadily to prevent curdling. Mix in the scallops and sautéed vegetables. Taste for seasoning. Divide the mixture among 12 scallop shells or ramekins. Freeze 6, then wrap, seal, label, and return to freezer.

FOR TONIGHT'S DINNER
Sprinkle the remaining 6 shells with the bread crumbs; dot with a little butter. Bake in a 425° oven 10 minutes, or until browned.

Arrange the frozen shells on a baking sheet; sprinkle the tops with bread crumbs and dot with butter. Bake in a 400° oven 20 minutes, or until hot and browned.

Serves 6 each time.

FRIED CLAMS

2 quarts shucked, shelled, soft clams
3 eggs
¼ cup water
1½ cups dry bread crumbs
2 teaspoons salt
½ teaspoon white pepper
Fat for deep frying

Wash the clams under running water until free of sand. Drain well, and cut away the black skin of the neck. Dip in the eggs beaten with the water, then in the bread crumbs mixed with the salt and pepper. Repeat the dipping process. Let dry 15 minutes.

Heat the fat to 375°. Fry half the clams 2 minutes. Drain and cool. Pack in freezer containers with freezer paper or foil between the layers. Seal, label, and freeze.

FOR TONIGHT'S DINNER
Fry the remaining clams 5 minutes. Drain and serve hot.

TO SERVE FROM FROZEN STATE
Arrange frozen clams on a baking sheet. Bake in a preheated 425° oven 10 minutes.

Serves 4 each time.

LOBSTER À L'AMÉRICAINE

4 1½-pound live lobsters
3 tablespoons olive oil
3 tablespoons butter
¾ cup chopped onions
½ cup grated carrots
½ teaspoon thyme
2 tablespoons minced parsley
¼ cup cognac
1 cup dry white wine
¾ cup canned tomato sauce
3 tomatoes, peeled and chopped
1½ teaspoons salt
¼ teaspoon freshly ground black pepper
1 clove garlic, minced
¼ teaspoon tarragon

Have the lobsters split and claws cracked. Remove the tail meat and cut each in 3 pieces. Remove the claw meat and cut in pieces. Reserve the shells.

Heat the oil in a deep skillet; sauté the lobster meat 5 minutes. Remove. Add the butter to the skillet; sauté the onions and carrots 5 minutes. Add the thyme, parsley, and shells. Heat the cognac and pour it into the skillet; set aflame. When flames die, add the wine, tomato sauce, tomatoes, salt, and pepper. Cover and cook over low heat 25 minutes. Discard the shells. Combine half the sauce with half the lobster. Chill quickly and pack into a freezer container. Seal, label, and freeze.

FOR TONIGHT'S DINNER

Combine the remaining lobster with the remaining sauce and add the garlic and tarragon. Cook over low heat 10 minutes. Taste for seasoning.

Turn into a saucepan; cover and cook over low heat until thawed. Mix in 1 minced clove garlic and ¼ teaspoon tarragon; heat and taste for seasoning.

Serves 2–4 each time.

STUFFED LOBSTER TAILS

8 lobster tails, cooked and drained
4 tablespoons butter
4 tablespoons flour
2 teaspoons salt
¼ teaspoon white pepper
½ teaspoon dry mustard
2 cups chicken broth
3 hard-cooked egg yolks, chopped
¼ cup dry bread crumbs
2 tablespoons melted butter

Remove the meat of the lobster tails and dice. Reserve the shells. Melt the butter in a saucepan; blend in the flour, salt, pepper, and mustard. Gradually add the broth, stirring steadily to the boiling point. Cook over low heat 5 minutes. Cool, then stir in the lobster and egg yolks. Taste for seasoning. Stuff the shells. Freeze 4; wrap, seal, label, and return to freezer.

FOR TONIGHT'S DINNER
Sprinkle the remaining lobster tails with the bread crumbs mixed with the melted butter. Bake in a preheated 375° oven 15 minutes, or until browned.

TO SERVE FROM FROZEN STATE
Unwrap lobster tails and sprinkle with ¼ cup bread crumbs mixed with 2 tablespoons melted butter. Bake in a preheated 325° oven 35 minutes, or until hot and browned.

Serves 4 each time.

LOBSTER NEWBURG

3 1¼-pound live lobsters or 1½ pounds cooked lobster meat
2 cups dry white wine
2 quarts water
4 teaspoons salt
2 bay leaves
¼ pound butter
4 tablespoons flour
¼ teaspoon paprika
¼ teaspoon nutmeg
2 cups light cream
2 cups milk
⅓ cup dry sherry
4 egg yolks
2 tablespoons minced parsley

If live lobsters are used, wash them. Combine and bring to a boil the wine, water, 2 teaspoons salt, and the bay leaves. Plunge the lobsters into the court bouillon and cook 15 minutes. Drain, cool, remove the meat and cube it. (Or cube cooked lobster meat.)

Melt the butter in a saucepan; blend in the flour, paprika, nutmeg, and remaining salt. Gradually add the cream, milk, and sherry, stirring steadily to the boiling point. Cook over low heat 5 minutes. Beat the egg yolks in a bowl; gradually add the hot sauce, stirring steadily to prevent curdling. Mix in the lobster. Return half the mixture to the saucepan, but not on the heat. Place the bowl in cold water or over ice to cool quickly. Pack into a container; seal, label, and freeze.

FOR TONIGHT'S DINNER

Heat the remaining lobster, stirring steadily, but do not let boil. Taste for seasoning and sprinkle with the parsley.

TO SERVE FROM FROZEN STATE

Turn into the top of a double boiler. Cover and place over hot water; cook until thawed. Remove cover and cook, stirring frequently, until hot but not boiling. Taste for seasoning and sprinkle with 2 tablespoons minced parsley.

Serves 4–6 each time.

SHRIMP WITH ALMONDS

¼ pound butter
1½ cups chopped onions
4 pounds raw shrimp, shelled and deveined
2½ teaspoons salt
½ teaspoon thyme
3 tablespoons minced parsley
2 cups dry white wine
1 cup peeled chopped tomatoes
½ cup heavy cream
¾ cup sliced blanched almonds

Melt the butter in a skillet; sauté the onions 10 minutes. Add the shrimp, salt, thyme, and parsley; sauté 2 minutes. Add the wine and tomatoes; cover and cook over low heat 5 minutes. Transfer half the mixture to a bowl; place in cold water or over ice to cool quickly. Pack into a container; seal, label, and freeze.

FOR TONIGHT'S DINNER
Cook the remaining shrimp 5 minutes longer. Stir in the cream and almonds. Heat and taste for seasoning.

TO SERVE FROM FROZEN STATE
Turn frozen shrimp into the top of a double boiler. Cook over hot water until thawed, then place over direct low heat. Stir in ½ cup heavy cream and ¾ cup sliced blanched almonds. Heat and taste for seasoning.

Serves 4–6 each time.

SHRIMP CREOLE

5 pounds raw shrimp, shelled and deveined
⅓ cup olive or salad oil
2 cups chopped onions
2 cups chopped green peppers
2 cups chopped celery
2 No. 3½ cans Italian-style tomatoes
2 8-ounce cans tomato sauce
2 teaspoons salt
¾ teaspoon freshly ground black pepper
2 cloves
2 allspice
4 bay leaves
1 clove garlic, minced

Wash and drain the shrimp. Heat half the oil in a skillet; sauté the shrimp 5 minutes. Drain and reserve.

Heat the remaining oil in a heavy saucepan; sauté the onions, green peppers, celery 15 minutes, stirring frequently. Mix in the tomatoes, tomato sauce, salt, and pepper. Tie the cloves, allspice, and bay leaves in a cheesecloth bag and add. Bring to a boil and cook over low heat 30 minutes. Discard the spice bag.

Remove two thirds of the sauce and cool. Add two thirds of the shrimp. Divide between 2 freezer containers. Cover, seal, label, and freeze.

FOR TONIGHT'S DINNER
Add the garlic and remaining shrimp to the remaining sauce. Cook over low heat 15 minutes. Taste for seasoning.

TO SERVE FROM FROZEN STATE
Turn contents of one container into a saucepan. Cover and cook over very low heat 10 minutes. Stir in 1 minced clove garlic. Cook, uncovered, 15 minutes longer, or until very hot. Taste for seasoning.
Serves 4–6 each time.

SHRIMP IN WINE SAUCE

6 tablespoons butter
1 cup chopped onions
1 cup grated carrots
2 tablespoons minced parsley
1 clove garlic, minced
2 tablespoons flour
2 cups diced peeled tomatoes
1¼ teaspoons salt
½ teaspoon thyme
1 bay leaf
4 pounds raw shrimp, shelled and deveined
4 tablespoons warm cognac
2 cups dry white wine
½ teaspoon freshly ground black pepper

Melt 4 tablespoons butter in a saucepan; sauté the onions, carrots, parsley, and garlic for 15 minutes, stirring frequently. Mix in the flour, then the tomatoes, salt, thyme, bay leaf, and shrimp. Cook over low heat 2 minutes, stirring constantly. Pour in the cognac and set aflame. When flames die, add the wine. Cook over medium heat 5 minutes. Transfer half the mixture to a bowl; place in cold water or over ice to cool quickly. Pack into a freezer container; seal, label, and freeze.

FOR TONIGHT'S DINNER
Add the pepper and remaining butter to the remaining shrimp; cook over high heat 7 minutes longer. Taste for seasoning.

TO SERVE FROM FROZEN STATE
Turn into a saucepan, cover, and cook over low heat 10 minutes. Stir in ½ teaspoon freshly ground black pepper and 2 tablespoons butter. Cook, uncovered, over medium heat 10 minutes, or until very hot. Taste for seasoning.
Serves 4–6 each time.

FISH CAKES

    3 pounds cod, halibut, or sole
    1 onion
    3 cups water
    1 bay leaf
    4 teaspoons salt
    ¾ teaspoon white pepper
    3 cups hot mashed potatoes
    6 eggs, beaten
    ½ teaspoon nutmeg
    1 cup dry bread crumbs
    Fat for deep frying

Wash the fish and combine with the onion, water, bay leaf, 2 teaspoons salt, and ¼ teaspoon pepper. Bring to a boil, cover, and cook over low heat 20 minutes. Drain and flake the fish very fine.

Mix together the fish, potatoes, eggs, nutmeg, and remaining salt and pepper. Shape into 24 balls and roll in the bread crumbs. Arrange 12 balls on a baking sheet and freeze. When frozen, wrap, seal, label, and return to freezer.

FOR TONIGHT'S DINNER

Heat the fat to 390° and fry the remaining balls until golden brown. Drain and serve with a tomato sauce.

TO SERVE FROM FROZEN STATE

Heat deep fat to 380°. Fry the balls in it until golden brown. Drain.

Serves 6 each time.

FISH ROLLS

1 pound tomatoes
3 teaspoons salt
¾ teaspoon pepper
12 fillets of sole
6 tablespoons butter
¾ cup dry white wine
3 tablespoons chopped onions
2 tablespoons flour
½ cup cognac
2 cups heavy cream

Peel and dice the tomatoes. Season with 1 teaspoon salt and ¼ teaspoon pepper and cook over low heat for 20 minutes, stirring frequently.

Season the fillets with the remaining salt and pepper and spread each with a little of the tomatoes (reserve 2 tablespoons). Roll up and fasten with thread or toothpicks. Arrange the rolls in a buttered casserole and dot each with a teaspoon of the butter. Add the wine and bring to a boil. Cover and cook over low heat 10 minutes. Remove the rolls and reserve the stock.

Melt the remaining butter in a skillet; sauté the onions 3 minutes. Blend in the flour, then the cognac, stock, and the remaining tomato mixture. Cook over medium heat 10 minutes. Mix in the cream and cook over low heat 10 minutes. Taste for seasoning. Arrange 6 rolls in a freezer container and pour half the sauce over them. Chill; cover, seal, label, and freeze.

FOR TONIGHT'S DINNER
Arrange the remaining rolls in a baking dish with the remaining sauce over them. Bake in a 450° oven 5 minutes.

TO SERVE FROM FROZEN STATE
Turn into a shallow casserole, cover, and bake in a 325° oven 15 minutes. Remove cover, raise heat to 425°, and bake 10 minutes longer, or until very hot.

Serves 6 each time.

BAKED FISH, NEW ORLEANS STYLE

8 slices sea bass, whitefish, etc.
3 teaspoons salt
¾ teaspoon freshly ground black pepper
4 tablespoons salad oil
¾ cup dry white wine
1 cup chopped green peppers
1 cup chopped onions
1 29-ounce can tomatoes
¼ teaspoon basil
1 tablespoon cornstarch
2 tablespoons water
1 cup soft bread crumbs
2 tablespoons melted butter

Wash and dry the fish; rub with 2 teaspoons salt, ½ teaspoon pepper, and 2 tablespoons of the oil. Let stand 15 minutes. Arrange in a greased baking dish and add the wine. Bake in a 400° oven 25 minutes, basting occasionally. Cool 4 slices.

Meanwhile heat the remaining oil in a saucepan; sauté the peppers and onions 5 minutes. Stir in the tomatoes, basil, and the remaining salt and pepper. Cover and cook over low heat 30 minutes. Mix the cornstarch and water; stir into the sauce until thickened. Remove half the sauce and cool. Arrange the slices of cooled fish and the cooled sauce in a container; seal, label, and freeze.

FOR TONIGHT'S DINNER

Pour the remaining sauce over the remaining fish. Toss the bread crumbs with the butter and sprinkle over the top. Bake in a 400° oven 15 minutes.

TO SERVE FROM FROZEN STATE

Turn into a baking dish. Cover and bake in a 325° oven 15 minutes. Remove cover and sprinkle with 1 cup soft bread crumbs tossed with 2 tablespoons melted butter. Raise heat to 400° and bake 15 minutes longer.

Serves 4 each time.

FISH IN WINE SAUCE

¼ pound butter
12 fillets of sole or slices fish
4 tablespoons chopped onions
2 teaspoons salt
¼ teaspoon white pepper
1½ cups dry white wine
2 cups clam juice
4 tablespoons flour
2 cups milk
1 cup heavy cream
½ cup chopped mushrooms

Melt 2 tablespoons butter in a large deep skillet; arrange the fish in it. Sprinkle with the onions, 1 teaspoon salt, the pepper, and add the wine and clam juice. Bring to a boil, cover, and cook over low heat 20 minutes. Remove the fish. Cook the stock over high heat 5 minutes.

Melt 4 tablespoons butter in a saucepan; blend in the flour, then the milk, cream, stock, and remaining salt, stirring steadily to the boiling point. Cook over low heat 5 minutes. Remove and cool half the sauce. Arrange 6 pieces of fish in a freezer container and cover with the cooled sauce. Cover, seal, label, and freeze.

FOR TONIGHT'S DINNER

Sauté the mushrooms 5 minutes in the remaining butter. Add to the remaining sauce and then arrange the fish in it. Heat and taste for seasoning.

TO SERVE FROM FROZEN STATE

Turn into a baking dish. Cover and bake in a preheated 375° oven until thawed. Mix in ½ cup chopped mushrooms sautéed in 2 tablespoons butter. Bake, uncovered, 5 minutes or until very hot. Taste for seasoning.

Serves 6 each time.

FISH MOUSSE

3½ pounds salmon, sole, pike, or halibut
2 tablespoons butter
1 tablespoon flour
2½ teaspoons salt
½ teaspoon white pepper
1 teaspoon dry mustard
⅛ teaspoon nutmeg
¾ cup milk
6 egg yolks
¼ cup cognac
3 egg whites, stiffly beaten
2 cups heavy cream, whipped

Discard the skin and bones of the fish. Grind the fish in a food chopper, using the finest blade, then chop until very smooth and fine. Or grind in an electric blender.

Melt the butter in a saucepan; blend in the flour, salt, pepper, mustard, and nutmeg. Gradually add the milk, stirring steadily to the boiling point. Cook over low heat 5 minutes. Beat the egg yolks and cognac in a bowl and gradually add the hot sauce, stirring steadily to prevent curdling. Mix in the fish, then fold in the egg whites and whipped cream. Turn into 2 buttered 1½-quart casseroles. Place in a shallow pan of hot water and bake in a preheated 350° oven 35 minutes. Remove 1 casserole; cool, and then chill it in the refrigerator. Wrap, seal, label, and freeze.

FOR TONIGHT'S DINNER

Continue baking the remaining casserole 15 minutes, or until firm. Carefully turn out. Serve with a sauce, if desired.

TO SERVE FROM FROZEN STATE

Unwrap casserole and place in a shallow pan of warm water; bake in a 325° oven 40 minutes, or until hot and firm.

Serves 4–6 each time.

POULTRY

There are so many ways to prepare poultry, and almost all freeze well.

Cooked turkey, chicken, duck, and so forth may be frozen on the carcass. If the bird is stuffed, carefully scoop out every bit of it and freeze it separately—stuffing does not freeze completely in the cavity of the bird. The exceptions are squabs, Rock Cornish hens, or other small birds. To serve the poultry cold, thaw while wrapped for 3 to 8 hours, depending upon the size. To serve hot, unwrap, place in a roasting pan, and roast in a 350° oven for 30 minutes to 1½ hours, also depending on the size of the bird. Keep up to 3 months.

Sliced poultry is best frozen when covered with gravy or sauce. Seal, label, and freeze. Reheat in the original container (if heat-proof, or if this food is in aluminum foil) or in double boiler or saucepan until hot. Stir gravy or sauce frequently. Keep no longer than 3 months.

CHICKEN FINANCIÈRE

3 3½-pound fryers, disjointed
1 tablespoon salt
¾ teaspoon freshly ground black pepper
¼ pound butter
4 tablespoons flour
2 cups dry sherry
2 cups fresh or canned chicken broth
4 chicken livers, cubed
1 cup sliced mushrooms
½ cup sliced green olives

Wash and dry the chicken; season with the salt and pepper. Melt 4 tablespoons butter in a skillet and brown the chicken in it. Mix the flour with a little sherry until smooth and add to the chicken with the remaining sherry and the broth. Cover and cook over low heat 20 minutes. Transfer two thirds of the mixture to a bowl or saucepan; place in cold water or over ice to cool quickly. Pack into 2 containers; seal, label, and freeze.

FOR TONIGHT'S DINNER

Sauté the livers in the remaining butter for 5 minutes. Remove livers and sauté the mushrooms 5 minutes. Add the livers, mushrooms, and olives to the chicken. Cover and cook over low heat 15 minutes, or until chicken is tender. Taste for seasoning.

TO SERVE FROM FROZEN STATE

Turn contents of one container into a saucepan or casserole. Cover and cook over low heat 20 minutes. Sauté 4 cubed chicken livers in 4 tablespoons butter 5 minutes. Remove livers and sauté 1 cup sliced mushrooms 5 minutes. Add the livers, mushrooms, and ½ cup sliced green olives to the chicken. Re-cover and cook over low heat 20 minutes, or until chicken is tender and hot. Taste for seasoning.

Serves 4–5 each time.

CHICKEN IN SPICY SAUCE

    3 3-pound fryers, disjointed
    1 tablespoon salt
    1 teaspoon freshly ground black pepper
    ⅓ cup flour
    4 tablespoons olive oil
    2 cups chopped onions
    2 cups dry white wine
    2 tablespoons tomato paste
    1 cup fresh or canned chicken broth
    ½ cup wine vinegar
    2 cloves garlic, minced
    2 teaspoons anchovy paste
    1 tablespoon capers
    3 tablespoons chopped sweet pickles
    2 tablespoons minced parsley

Wash and dry the chicken; toss each piece in a mixture of the salt, pepper, and flour. Heat the oil in a Dutch oven or casserole; sauté the onions 10 minutes. Add the chicken and brown well. Mix in the wine, tomato paste, and broth. Cover and cook over medium heat 35 minutes.

Transfer two thirds of the chicken mixture to a bowl or saucepan; place in cold water or over ice to cool quickly. Pack into 2 containers; seal, label, and freeze.

FOR TONIGHT'S DINNER

Continue cooking the remaining chicken 15 minutes, or until tender. Cook the vinegar in a small saucepan until reduced to half; add the garlic, anchovy paste, capers, pickles, and parsley. Cook 1 minute. Pour over chicken and serve.

TO SERVE FROM FROZEN STATE

Turn contents of one container into a casserole; cover and place in a 375° oven for 45 minutes, or until hot and tender. Prepare vinegar mixture as above; pour over chicken and serve.

Serves 4 each time.

CHICKEN PAPRIKA

3 3½-pound fryers, disjointed
1 tablespoon salt
½ teaspoon freshly ground black pepper
6 tablespoons butter
4 cups diced onions
2 tablespoons sweet paprika
1½ cups fresh or canned chicken broth
¾ cup sour cream

Wash and dry the chicken; rub with the salt and pepper. Melt the butter in a Dutch oven or heavy saucepan; brown the chicken in it. Remove. Stir the onions into the pan and cook over low heat 15 minutes, mixing frequently. Blend in the paprika. Return the chicken and add the broth; cover and cook over low heat 20 minutes.

Transfer two thirds of the mixture to a bowl or saucepan and place in cold water or over ice to cool quickly. Pack into 2 containers; seal, label, and freeze.

FOR TONIGHT'S DINNER

Re-cover pan and cook over low heat 20 minutes longer, or until tender. Stir in the sour cream; heat but do not let boil. Taste for seasoning.

TO SERVE FROM FROZEN STATE

Turn contents of one container into a saucepan, cover, and cook over low heat 40 minutes, or until hot and tender. Stir in ¾ cup sour cream; heat but do not let boil. Taste for seasoning.

Serves 4 each time.

CHICKEN IN RED WINE

3 4-pound pullets, disjointed
1 tablespoon salt
¾ teaspoon freshly ground black pepper
1 teaspoon paprika
¼ teaspoon nutmeg
½ cup flour
¼ pound salt pork or bacon, diced
1½ pounds small white onions
⅓ cup warm cognac
4 cups dry red wine
1 pound small mushrooms
½ teaspoon thyme
½ teaspoon marjoram
2 bay leaves
1 tablespoon potato flour

Wash and dry the chicken; toss each piece in a mixture of the salt, pepper, paprika, nutmeg, and flour.

Brown the salt pork in a Dutch oven or casserole; sauté the onions until golden. Remove. To the fat which remains, add the chicken; cook over high heat until very brown. Pour off the fat. Add the cognac and set aflame. When flames die, add the wine, mushrooms, thyme, marjoram, bay leaves, and onions. Cook over low heat 45 minutes.

Transfer two thirds of the chicken mixture to a bowl or saucepan; place in cold water or over ice to cool quickly. Pack into 2 containers; seal, label, and freeze.

FOR TONIGHT'S DINNER

Continue cooking the remaining chicken 20 minutes, or until tender. Mix the potato flour with 3 tablespoons water and stir into the gravy. Cook over low heat until thickened. Taste for seasoning.

TO SERVE FROM FROZEN STATE

Turn contents of one container into a casserole; cover and place in a 350° oven for 45 minutes or until very hot. Thicken gravy, if necessary, with 2 teaspoons potato flour mixed with 2 tablespoons water.

Serves 4–5 each time.

CHICKEN CROQUETTES
Suprême de Volaille Pojarski

6 chicken breasts
2 cups cubed white bread
1 cup heavy cream
⅜ pound (¾ cup) butter
2½ teaspoons salt
¾ teaspoon white pepper
1 cup dry bread crumbs

Remove the skin and bones of the chicken; grind the meat in a food chopper or chop very fine. (There should be 6 cups.) Soak the bread in the cream for 10 minutes, mash smooth and blend into the chicken. Melt half the butter; add to the chicken with the salt and pepper. Shape the mixture into 12 croquettes; dip in the crumbs.

Melt half the remaining butter in a skillet; sauté 6 croquettes until lightly browned on both sides. Cool, wrap, label, and freeze.

FOR IMMEDIATE SERVICE

Add the remaining butter to the skillet; sauté the remaining croquettes until browned on both sides and cooked through.

Serve with hollandaise sauce, if desired.

TO SERVE FROM FROZEN STATE

Melt 4 tablespoons butter in a skillet; sauté the croquettes until hot and cooked through.

Serves 6 each time.

STUFFED CORNISH HENS OR SQUABS

2 cups wild rice
5 cups canned chicken broth
⅜ pound (1½ sticks) butter
2 cups chopped onions
½ pound mushrooms, chopped
1 tablespoon Worcestershire sauce
1 teaspoon freshly ground black pepper
12 Rock Cornish hens or squabs
1½ tablespoons salt
2 teaspoons paprika
24 small white onions
2 cups dry white wine
3 tablespoons cognac

Wash the wild rice thoroughly and drain well. Combine in a saucepan with the broth; cover, bring to a boil, and cook over low heat 20 minutes. Drain if any liquid remains.

Melt half the butter in a skillet; sauté the onions and mushrooms 10 minutes. Add the wild rice, Worcestershire sauce, and ½ teaspoon pepper.

Season the hens with the salt, paprika, and remaining pepper; stuff, sew or skewer the openings, and truss. Melt the remaining butter in a shallow roasting pan. Brown the birds and whole onions over medium heat. Add the wine; roast in a 375° oven 35 minutes, basting frequently. Transfer 8 hens and two thirds of the gravy and onions into a bowl or pan. Place in cold water or over ice to cool quickly. Arrange in 2 containers (or more, as you like); seal, label, and freeze.

FOR TONIGHT'S DINNER
Continue roasting the remaining birds 20 minutes, or until tender. Arrange on a serving dish with pan gravy around them. Heat the cognac, pour over the hens, set aflame, and serve.

Arrange hens in a shallow pan. Cover with aluminum foil. Bake in a 300° oven 25 minutes. Remove foil, increase heat to 375°, and bake 20 minutes longer or until hot and tender, basting frequently. Be sure the stuffing is hot. Pour 3 tablespoons warmed cognac over them and set aflame.

FRIED CHICKEN

4 2½-pound fryers, disjointed
1 cup sifted flour
2½ teaspoons salt
½ teaspoon white pepper
3 eggs, beaten
4 tablespoons water
1 cup dry bread crumbs
½ cup crushed corn flakes
1 cup shortening, oil, or butter

Wash and dry the chickens; roll in a mixture of the flour, salt, and pepper. Beat the eggs and water together; mix the crumbs and corn flakes together. Dip the chicken in the eggs and then roll in the crumb mixture.

Melt the fat in a skillet; sauté the chicken until very lightly browned on all sides, about 10 minutes. Transfer half the chicken to a bowl; place in cold water or over ice to cool quickly. Pack into 1 or 2 containers; seal, label and freeze.

FOR TONIGHT'S DINNER
Continue sautéing the remaining chicken 30 minutes, or until tender and browned; turn pieces frequently. Drain well.

TO SERVE FROM FROZEN STATE
Melt 4 tablespoons of fat in a skillet; arrange the chicken in it. Bake in a 350° oven 40 minutes, or until tender and browned; turn pieces frequently.

Each chicken serves 4.

CHICKEN AND OLIVES

3 3½-pound fryers, disjointed
½ cup flour
2½ teaspoons salt
½ teaspoon freshly ground black pepper
2 tablespoons olive oil
3 tablespoons butter
1¼ cups chopped onions
⅓ cup cognac
1½ cups dry white wine
1½ cups diced tomatoes
2 bay leaves
½ teaspoon marjoram
1 clove garlic, minced
¼ pound mushrooms, quartered
¼ cup sliced stuffed green olives
2 tablespoons minced parsley

Wash and dry the chicken; toss each part in a mixture of the flour, salt, and pepper. Heat the olive oil and butter in a Dutch oven or casserole; brown the chicken and onions in it. Add the cognac, wine, tomatoes, bay leaves, and marjoram. Cover and cook over low heat 25 minutes. Transfer two thirds of the chicken and sauce to a bowl or saucepan; place in cold water or over ice to cool quickly. Pack into 2 containers; seal, label, and freeze.

FOR TONIGHT'S DINNER
Add the garlic and mushrooms to the remaining chicken. Cover and cook 15 minutes. Stir in the olives; cook 5 minutes or until chicken is tender. Taste for seasoning and sprinkle with the parsley.

Turn contents of one container into a casserole, cover, and cook over low heat 20 minutes. Add 1 minced clove garlic and ¼ pound quartered mushrooms; re-cover and cook 20 minutes. Stir in ¼ cup sliced stuffed olives; cook 5 minutes or until very hot. Taste for seasoning and sprinkle with 2 tablespoons minced parsley.

Serves 4–5 each time.

CHICKEN À LA KING

¼ pound butter
½ pound mushrooms, sliced
⅓ cup flour
1 teaspoon salt
⅛ teaspoon white pepper
2¼ cups chicken broth
1 cup light cream
4 cups cubed cooked chicken or turkey
2 pimentos, cut julienne
3 tablespoons dry sherry

Melt the butter in a saucepan; sauté the mushrooms 5 minutes. Blend in the flour, salt, and pepper until smooth. Gradually add the broth and cream, stirring steadily to the boiling point; cook over low heat 5 minutes. Pour half the mixture into a bowl and add half the poultry, pimentos, and sherry. Place in cold water or over ice to cool quickly. Pack into a container; seal, label, and freeze.

FOR TONIGHT'S DINNER
Add the remaining poultry, pimentos, and sherry to the remaining sauce; cook over low heat 5 minutes. Taste for seasoning.

TO SERVE FROM FROZEN STATE
Turn into the top of a double boiler. Place over hot water, cover, and cook until thawed and hot. Taste for seasoning.

Serves 4 each time.

CHICKEN CACCIATORA

3 3-pound fryers, disjointed
1 tablespoon salt
½ teaspoon freshly ground black pepper
½ cup flour
⅓ cup olive oil
1½ cups chopped onions
3 cups drained canned tomatoes
½ cup dry white wine
¾ teaspoon oregano
2 tablespoons bay leaves
1 clove garlic, minced
½ cup diced green peppers
½ cup sliced mushrooms
2 tablespoons butter

Wash and dry the chicken; toss in a mixture of the salt, pepper, and flour. Heat the oil in a Dutch oven or casserole; brown the chicken in it. Add the onions and let brown. Stir in the tomatoes, wine, oregano, and bay leaves. Cover and cook over low heat 20 minutes. Transfer two thirds of the mixture to a bowl or saucepan; place in cold water or over ice to cool quickly. Pack into 2 containers; seal, label, and freeze.

FOR TONIGHT'S DINNER
Sauté the garlic, peppers, and mushrooms in the butter 5 minutes; add to the remaining chicken. Cover and cook over low heat 20 minutes or until tender. Taste for seasoning.

TO SERVE FROM FROZEN STATE
Turn contents of one container into a casserole, cover, and cook over low heat 20 minutes. Sauté 1 minced clove garlic, ½ cup diced green peppers, and ½ cup sliced mushrooms in 2 tablespoons butter for 5 minutes. Add to the chicken; re-cover and cook over low heat 20 minutes, or until hot and tender. Taste for seasoning. Serves 4–5 each time.

SMOTHERED CHICKEN

4 2-pound broilers, disjointed
½ cup flour
1 tablespoon salt
¾ teaspoon freshly ground black pepper
¼ pound butter
3 cups hot light cream
1 pound broad noodles, cooked and drained
¼ cup dry bread crumbs

Wash and dry the chicken; toss each part in a mixture of the flour, salt, and pepper. (Reserve any remaining flour.)

Melt 6 tablespoons butter in a skillet; brown the chicken in it on all sides. Cover and cook over low heat 15 minutes. Remove the chicken. To the fat remaining in the skillet, blend in the reserved flour. (If you haven't any left, use 2 tablespoons.) Gradually add the cream, stirring steadily to the boiling point. Scrape the skillet of all particles and cook over low heat 5 minutes. Taste for seasoning.

Arrange the noodles in 2 casseroles and place the chicken over it. Pour the sauce over all. Cool, wrap, seal, label, and freeze.

FOR TONIGHT'S DINNER

Sprinkle the bread crumbs on the remaining casserole and dot with the remaining butter. Bake in a 350° oven 25 minutes, or until chicken is tender and sauce bubbling.

TO SERVE FROM FROZEN STATE

Unwrap casserole and bake, covered, in a 300° oven 20 minutes. Uncover, sprinkle with ¼ cup dry bread crumbs, and dot with 2 tablespoons butter. Raise heat to 350° and bake 25 minutes, or until chicken is tender and sauce very hot.

Serves 4–6 each time.

Note: Chicken may be removed from bone before placing in casserole, if you prefer.

CHICKEN TARRAGON

3 4-pound pullets, disjointed
4 tablespoons salt
¾ teaspoon freshly ground black pepper
½ cup flour
¼ pound butter
2 cups chopped onions
Bunch tarragon, minced, or 1 tablespoon dried
1 cup dry white wine
1 cup fresh or canned chicken broth

Wash and dry the chicken; toss with a mixture of the salt, pepper, and flour. Melt the butter in a Dutch oven or heavy saucepan; brown the chicken and onions in it. Add the tarragon, wine, and broth; cover and cook over low heat 1 hour. Transfer two thirds of the chicken and gravy to a bowl or saucepan. Place in cold water or over ice to cool quickly. Pack into 2 containers; seal, label, and freeze.

FOR TONIGHT'S DINNER

Continue cooking the remaining chicken, uncovered, 30 minutes or until tender. There will not be much gravy, but the chicken will be glazed with it.

TO SERVE FROM FROZEN STATE

Turn the contents of one container into a casserole or baking dish. Cover and place in a 350° oven for 20 minutes. Uncover and bake 20 minutes longer, or until very hot and chicken is tender. Taste for seasoning.

Serves 4–5 each time.

CHICKEN STEW

1 tablespoon salt
1 teaspoon pepper
1 tablespoon Spanish paprika
4 3½-pound fryers, disjointed
½ cup olive or salad oil
2 cups diced onions
2 bay leaves
1 cup dry white wine
2 cloves garlic, minced
4 potatoes, pared and cubed
1 No. 1 can tiny peas, drained
½ cup sliced green olives
½ cup sliced pimentos

Combine the salt, pepper, and paprika. Season the chickens with the mixture.

Heat the oil in a skillet. Brown the chickens in it, then transfer to a casserole or heavy saucepan. Sauté the onions in the fat remaining in the skillet for 10 minutes. Add to the chicken with the bay leaves and wine. Cover and cook over low heat 1 hour. Transfer half the mixture to a bowl or saucepan; place in cold water or over ice to cool quickly. Pack in a freezer container; seal, label, and freeze.

FOR TONIGHT'S DINNER

Add the garlic and potatoes to the remaining chicken. Cover and cook over low heat 15 minutes. (Add a little water if necessary.) Add the peas, olives, and pimentos. Cook 15 minutes. Taste for seasoning.

TO SERVE FROM FROZEN STATE

Turn into a saucepan, add 2 minced cloves garlic and 4 pared, half-cooked, cubed potatoes. Cover and cook over low heat 30 minutes. Add 1 can drained peas, ½ cup sliced green olives, and ½ cup sliced pimentos. Cook 10 minutes. Correct seasoning.

Serves 6–8 each time.

CHICKEN CHOW MEIN

2 4-pound chickens, disjointed
1 onion
2 stalks celery
3 sprigs parsley
1 bay leaf
1 tablespoon salt
½ teaspoon white pepper
8 cups water
3 tablespoons peanut or salad oil
1½ cups thinly sliced onions
2 cups sliced celery
1 pound sliced mushrooms
2½ tablespoons cornstarch
⅓ cup soy sauce
1 cup sliced bamboo shoots
2 cups sliced water chestnuts
2 cups bean sprouts

Wash the chickens; combine in a saucepan with the onion, celery, parsley, bay leaf, salt, pepper and water. Bring to a boil, cover loosely, and cook over low heat 1 hour, or until tender. Remove the chicken and cut into strips. Cook the broth over medium heat 30 minutes longer. Strain and measure 4 cups.

Heat the oil in a skillet; sauté the sliced onions, celery, and mushrooms 3 minutes. Add 2 cups broth and cook over low heat 10 minutes.

Mix the cornstarch until smooth with the soy sauce and remaining broth. Add to the skillet, mixing steadily. Add the bamboo shoots, water chestnuts, bean sprouts, and chicken. Cook 2 minutes. Transfer half the mixture to a bowl; place in cold water or over ice to cool quickly. Pack into a container; seal, label, and freeze.

FOR TONIGHT'S DINNER

Continue cooking the chow mein 10 minutes. Taste for seasoning and serve with fried noodles.

TO SERVE FROM FROZEN STATE

Turn into a saucepan; cover and cook over low heat until thawed. Uncover and cook until very hot. Taste for seasoning and serve with fried noodles.

Serves 6–8 each time.

FRIED NOODLES
(for Chow Mein)

3 quarts water
1 tablespoon salt
1 pound fine noodles
½ cup corn or peanut oil

Bring the water and salt to a boil; cook the noodles in it 8 minutes. Drain, rinse under cold water, and drain again. Place on 2 large round plates and chill 4 hours.

Heat ¼ cup oil in a large skillet; fry 1 plate of noodles until browned on both sides. Turn with a pancake turner to keep in 1 piece. Keep warm while frying the remaining noodles, or use 2 skillets.

CHICKEN TETRAZZINI

¾ pound spaghetti
¼ pound butter
1 pound mushrooms, sliced
5 tablespoons flour
3 cups fresh or canned chicken broth
1½ cups heavy cream
1½ teaspoons salt
½ teaspoon white pepper
⅛ teaspoon nutmeg
4 tablespoons dry sherry
½ cup grated Swiss cheese
4 cups cooked chicken or turkey, cut julienne
¼ cup grated Parmesan cheese

Cook the spaghetti in salted water 2 minutes less than package directs; drain.

Melt half the butter in a skillet; sauté the mushrooms 5 minutes. Melt the remaining butter in a saucepan; stir in the flour until smooth. Gradually add the broth and cream, stirring steadily to the boiling point. Cook over low heat 10 minutes. Stir in the salt, pepper, nutmeg, sherry, and Swiss cheese until cheese melts.

Mix half the sauce with the spaghetti and mushrooms; mix remaining sauce with the chicken. In 2 1½-quart casseroles, or 1 casserole and 1 freezer container, spread layers of the spaghetti mixture and chicken mixture. Place 1 casserole in cold water or over ice to cool quickly. Cover, seal, label, and freeze.

FOR TONIGHT'S DINNER

Sprinkle remaining casserole with the Parmesan cheese. Bake in a preheated 350° oven 20 minutes, or until browned.

TO SERVE FROM FROZEN STATE

Place covered casserole in a preheated 325° oven for 20 minutes. Remove cover, sprinkle with ¼ cup Parmesan cheese, and raise temperature to 350°. Bake 20 minutes, until browned and hot.

Serves 4–5 each time.

CHICKEN KIEV

6 chicken breasts
½ pound butter
4 tablespoons minced chives
½ cup flour
2½ teaspoons salt
½ teaspoon white pepper
4 eggs, beaten
1½ cups dry bread crumbs
Fat for deep frying

Buy the breasts of 3-pound fryers and have them cut in half. Carefully remove the skin and bones. Place each half between 2 sheets of waxed paper and pound as thin as possible with a cleaver or wooden mallet.

Cut the sticks of very cold butter in half lengthwise and then in thirds crosswise. Place 1 piece in the center of each piece of chicken; sprinkle with a little chives. Fold over one side of the chicken and then roll up and completely encase the butter.

Roll in a mixture of the flour, salt, and pepper, then dip in the eggs and roll in the bread crumbs. Freeze 6; wrap, seal, label, and return to freezer.

FOR TONIGHT'S DINNER

Chill the remaining 6 cutlets 1 hour. Heat the fat to 360° and fry the breasts in it until lightly browned. Drain and place on a baking sheet. Bake in a 400° oven 10 minutes.

TO SERVE FROM FROZEN STATE

Heat deep fat to 365°; fry the cutlets in it until delicately browned. Place on a baking sheet and bake in a 400° oven 15 minutes.

Serves 6 each time.

SPANISH CHICKEN AND RICE CASSEROLE

3 3-pound fryers, disjointed
4 teaspoons salt
¾ teaspoon freshly ground black pepper
⅓ cup flour
⅓ cup olive oil
2 cups diced onions
1½ cups drained canned tomatoes
4 cups fresh or canned chicken broth
2 bay leaves
¾ teaspoon saffron
3 cups raw rice
1 clove garlic, minced
¼ cup pimentos, cut julienne
2 tablespoons dry sherry

Wash and dry the chicken; toss each piece in a mixture of the salt, pepper, and flour. Heat the oil in a Dutch oven or casserole; brown the chicken in it. Add the onions and continue browning. Stir in the tomatoes, broth, bay leaves, and saffron. Cover and bake in a 350° oven 10 minutes. Add the rice; re-cover and bake 20 minutes.

Transfer two thirds of the mixture to a bowl or saucepan; place in cold water or over ice to cool quickly. Pack into 2 containers; seal, label, and freeze.

FOR TONIGHT'S DINNER
Add the garlic to the remaining chicken and rice. Re-cover and bake 20 minutes longer, or until chicken and rice are tender. Arrange the pimentos on the top and pour the sherry over all. Bake, uncovered, 5 minutes.

TO SERVE FROM FROZEN STATE
Turn contents of one container into a casserole; cover and place in a 325° oven for 20 minutes. Add 1 minced clove garlic; re-cover

and bake 25 minutes. Arrange ¼ cup julienne-cut pimentos on top and pour 2 tablespoons dry sherry over all. Bake, uncovered, 5 minutes or until very hot. Taste for seasoning.

Serves 4–6 each time.

CHICKEN IN CHAMPAGNE

¼ pound butter
2 cups thinly sliced onions
½ cup grated carrots
4 2-pound broilers, quartered
2½ teaspoons salt
½ teaspoon thyme
2 bay leaves
3 cups champagne or dry white wine
1 cup heavy cream

Melt the butter in a casserole; sauté the onions and carrots 5 minutes. Add the broilers; brown lightly. Add the salt, thyme, bay leaves, and champagne. Cover and bake in a preheated 350° oven 45 minutes. Transfer half the contents of the casserole to a bowl, place in cold water or over ice to cool quickly. Pack into a container; seal, label, and freeze.

FOR TONIGHT'S DINNER

Remove the chicken from the casserole. Stir the cream into the sauce, stirring constantly. Return the chicken and cook over low heat 5 minutes, or until tender. Taste for seasoning.

TO SERVE FROM FROZEN STATE

Turn into a casserole; bake in a preheated 350° oven 45 minutes, or until hot. Stir 1 cup heavy cream into the sauce. Bake 10 minutes longer. Taste for seasoning.

Serves 6 each time.

CHICKEN AND SWEETBREAD PIE

3 pair sweetbreads
¼ pound butter
2 4-pound roasting chickens, disjointed
2 cups thinly sliced onions
1 cup sliced carrots
4 teaspoons salt
¾ teaspoon freshly ground black pepper
2 cups sliced mushrooms
1 cup diced ham
⅓ cup cognac
½ cup Marsala or sweet sherry
2 cups heavy cream
Pastry for 2-crust pie

Wash the sweetbreads and soak in cold water to cover for 1 hour. Cook in lightly salted water 10 minutes. Drain; cover with cold water until cold. Drain, remove membranes, and dice; refrigerate until needed.

Melt half the butter in a Dutch oven; brown the chicken, onions, and carrots in it. Season with the salt and pepper. Cover and cook over low heat 45 minutes, shaking the pan and turning the pieces frequently. Add the remaining butter, mushrooms, ham, and the sweetbreads; cook 5 minutes. Stir in the cognac, wine, and cream. Cover and cook over low heat 20 minutes. Taste for seasoning.

Transfer half the mixture to a 2-quart casserole; place in cold water or over ice to cool quickly. Cover with half of the pastry, sealing the edges well. Wrap, seal, label, and freeze.

FOR TONIGHT'S DINNER
Preheat oven to 425°.
Turn the remaining chicken mixture into a 2-quart casserole and cover with the remaining pastry; make a few gashes in the top. Bake 25 minutes, or until pastry is browned.

Cut a few gashes in the pastry. Place in a preheated 400° oven for 50 minutes, or until browned and hot.

Serves 6–8 each time.

Note: The chicken can be removed from the bone, if you prefer.

CHICKEN OR TURKEY PIES

6 tablespoons butter
6 tablespoons flour
1 teaspoon salt
½ teaspoon freshly ground black pepper
3 cups chicken broth
4 cups cooked sliced chicken or turkey
2 cups cooked green peas
2 cups sliced sautéed mushrooms
2 cups cooked sliced carrots
Pastry for 2-crust pie

Melt the butter in a saucepan; blend in the flour, salt, and pepper. Gradually add the broth, stirring steadily to the boiling point. Cook over low heat 5 minutes. Cool. Add the poultry, peas, mushrooms, and carrots. Taste for seasoning. Divide the mixture between 2 1½-quart baking dishes or 10 individual 1½-cup baking dishes. Roll out dough and cut to fit the tops. Seal edges well.

Freeze the number you want to freeze; then wrap, seal, label, and return to the freezer.

FOR IMMEDIATE SERVICE
Cut a few slits in the pastry and brush with a little cream. Bake in a preheated 425° oven 35 minutes for a large pie, 25 minutes for small, or until browned.

TO SERVE FROM FROZEN STATE
Unwrap frozen pie or pies and cut a few slits in the top. Bake in a preheated 375° oven 50 minutes for large pie, 40 for small, or until browned.

CHICKEN PILAFF

2 5-pound pullets, disjointed
3 quarts water
1 onion
1 stalk celery
2 sprigs parsley
½ teaspoon thyme
1½ tablespoons salt
4 tablespoons olive oil
1½ cups chopped onion
3 cups raw rice
½ teaspoon saffron
½ teaspoon white pepper
1 cup seedless raisins
1 cup blanched sliced almonds

Combine the chicken, water, onion, celery, parsley, thyme, and 1 tablespoon salt in a saucepan. Bring to a boil, cover, and cook over low heat 1½ hours, or until chicken is tender. Remove the chicken and cut meat from the bones. Strain the stock and measure 5 cups; skim the fat.

Heat 2 tablespoons oil in a saucepan and sauté the chopped onions until yellow. Remove onions. Heat remaining oil in the saucepan; stir in the rice until well coated and yellow. Add the stock, saffron, pepper, sautéed onion, and remaining salt. Cover and cook over low heat 10 minutes. Divide the mixture in half. Mix half the chicken into one part and cool. Pack into a container; seal, label, and freeze.

FOR TONIGHT'S DINNER

Turn the other half of the rice into a casserole; add the remaining chicken and the raisins and nuts. Mix lightly. Bake in a 325° oven 30 minutes, or until rice is tender, adding a little more stock if casserole becomes dry.

TO SERVE FROM FROZEN STATE

Turn into a casserole. Bake in a 350° oven 25 minutes. Stir in 1 cup seedless raisins and 1 cup blanched sliced almonds. Bake uncovered 20 minutes, or until rice is tender. Add a little more chicken broth if casserole becomes dry.

Serves 6–7 each time.

WILD RICE CASSEROLE

2 cups wild rice
2 pounds mushrooms, sliced
1 cup chopped onions
⅜ pound (¾ cup) butter
3 teaspoons salt
½ teaspoon freshly ground black pepper
6 cups diced cooked turkey or chicken
1 cup blanched sliced almonds
6 cups canned chicken broth
2½ cups heavy cream

Wash the rice thoroughly. Cover with water, bring to a boil, remove from heat, and let soak 1 hour. Drain.

Sauté the mushrooms and onions in ½ cup of the butter until browned. Combine in a bowl with the wild rice, salt, pepper, poultry, almonds, broth, and cream. Mix lightly and turn into 2 buttered casseroles. Chill, wrap, seal, label, and freeze.

FOR TONIGHT'S DINNER

Dot the remaining casserole with the remaining butter. Bake in a 350° oven 1 hour, or until rice is tender and almost dry.

TO SERVE FROM FROZEN STATE

Place covered casserole in a 300° oven; bake 20 minutes. Uncover, raise heat to 350°, dot with 2 tablespoons butter, and bake 1 hour longer or until rice is tender.

Serves 6–8 each time.

CASSEROLE OF RICE AND POULTRY

6 tablespoons butter
2 cups thinly sliced onions
2 cups raw rice
4½ cups chicken broth
½ teaspoon thyme
2 bay leaves
3 sprigs parsley
6 cups diced cooked chicken or turkey
4 tablespoons flour
3 cups light cream
2 teaspoons salt
½ teaspoon white pepper
¾ cup grated Swiss or Gruyère cheese

Melt half the butter in a saucepan; sauté the onions 5 minutes. Stir in the rice until lightly browned. Add the broth, thyme, bay leaves, and parsley. Cover and cook over low heat 15 minutes, or until the liquid is absorbed and rice tender. Discard bay leaves and parsley; taste for seasoning. Pack the rice around the sides of 2 buttered 1½–2-quart casseroles; fill the center with the chicken.

Melt the remaining butter in a saucepan; blend in the flour. Gradually add the cream, stirring constantly to the boiling point. Add the salt, pepper, and 4 tablespoons cheese. Cook over low heat 5 minutes. Pour over the chicken. Chill 1 casserole; cover, wrap, seal, label, and freeze.

FOR TONIGHT'S DINNER
Sprinkle the remaining cheese on top of the remaining casserole; bake in a 400° oven 15 minutes or until browned.

TO SERVE FROM FROZEN STATE
Place covered casserole in a 350° oven for 15 minutes. Remove cover and sprinkle with ½ cup grated Swiss or Gruyère cheese. Raise heat to 400° and bake 15 minutes longer, or until browned and very hot.
Serves 4–6 each time.

CHICKEN FRITTERS

¼ pound butter
3 cups chicken broth
2 teaspoons salt
¾ teaspoon white pepper
2 cups sifted flour
6 eggs
2 cups ground cooked chicken
1 cup finely sliced blanched almonds
Fat for deep frying

Bring the butter, broth, salt, and pepper to a boil. Add the flour all at once, stirring steadily until mixture leaves the sides of the pan. Cool 3 minutes, then beat in 1 egg at a time, beating until smooth and shiny after each addition. Mix in the chicken and almonds. Taste for seasoning.

Shape into 20–24 balls between floured hands. Heat the fat to 375°. Fry half the balls 5 minutes. Drain and cool. Pack into a container; seal, label, and freeze.

FOR TONIGHT'S DINNER
Heat the fat to 380°. Fry the remaining balls 3 minutes. Increase temperature of fat to 390° and fry the balls until browned. Drain and serve hot.

TO SERVE FROM FROZEN STATE
Arrange the frozen balls on a greased baking sheet. Bake in a preheated 350° oven 25 minutes, or until browned and hot.
Serve 5–6 each time.

ROAST DUCK WITH CHERRIES

2 5–6 pound ducks
1 tablespoon salt
¾ teaspoon pepper
½ cup sugar
½ cup cider vinegar
2 tablespoons butter
¼ cup flour
1 cup fresh or canned chicken broth
1½ cups orange juice
¼ cup grated orange rind
¼ cup lemon juice
1 No. 2 can pitted bing cherries
2 tablespoons brandy

Clean the ducks thoroughly, wash, and dry. Rub the salt and pepper into them. Place on a rack in a shallow roasting pan and roast in a 475° oven 20 minutes. Pour off the fat. Reduce the heat to 350° and roast 1½ hours longer. Remove one duck and chill. Wrap in moisture- vaporproof wrap, seal, label, and freeze. Continue roasting the other duck 30 minutes longer or until tender, crisp, and brown.

Combine the sugar and vinegar in a saucepan; cook over low heat until mixture turns dark brown. In a separate saucepan, melt the butter and stir in the flour; gradually add the broth, stirring constantly to the boiling point. Add the orange juice, orange rind, lemon juice, juice of the canned cherries, the brandy, and allow to caramelize. Cook over low heat 10 minutes, stirring occasionally. Remove half the sauce and chill. Pour into a jar; seal, label, and freeze.

FOR TONIGHT'S DINNER
Add the cherries to the remaining sauce and heat. Carve the remaining duck and serve the sauce separately.

Place frozen duck on a rack in a shallow roasting pan. Roast in a 375° oven 1½ hours. Turn the sauce into a saucepan and heat. Add 1 cup drained cherries or 1 segmented orange.

Serves 4 each time.

ROAST DUCK WITH ORANGE SAUCE

Roast the ducks as directed in the preceding recipe, and prepare the following sauce:

1 cup sugar
2 cups currant jelly
3 cups orange juice
1 cup dry sherry
3 tablespoons cornstarch
1 cup water
2 oranges, peeled and segmented

Combine and bring to a boil the sugar, jelly, and orange juice. Cook over low heat 15 minutes. Stir in the sherry; cook 5 minutes. Blend the cornstarch with the water and mix into the sauce until it thickens. Pour half the sauce into a freezer container. Cool, seal, label, and freeze.

FOR TONIGHT'S DINNER
Add the oranges to the remaining sauce; cook 2 minutes. Serve in a sauceboat.

TO SERVE FROM FROZEN STATE
Turn into a saucepan and cook over low heat until hot. Add 2 peeled, segmented oranges; cook 2 minutes.

DUCK WITH PINEAPPLE

3 5-pound ducks, disjointed
1 No. 2 can pineapple chunks
1 cup soy sauce
¼ cup dry sherry
2 teaspoons salt
½ teaspoon Ac'cent
2 teaspoons powdered ginger
4 tablespoons peanut oil
1 clove garlic, minced
2 tablespoons butter

Wash the ducks thoroughly, remove as much fat as possible, and dry. Drain the pineapple and mix the juice with the soy sauce, sherry, salt, Ac'cent, and ginger. Marinate the duck in the mixture 3 hours, basting frequently. Drain, reserving the marinade.

Heat the oil in a roasting pan; brown the duck in it well. Pour off all the fat. Add the marinade; cover and bake in a 375° oven 45 minutes. Transfer 2 ducks and two thirds of the gravy to a bowl or saucepan. Place in cold water or over ice to cool quickly. Pack into 2 containers; seal, label, and freeze.

FOR TONIGHT'S DINNER

Add the garlic to the remaining duck. Bake, uncovered, 20 minutes longer or until tender, basting twice. Sauté the pineapple in the butter and arrange around the duck.

TO SERVE FROM FROZEN STATE

Turn contents of one container into a casserole, cover, and bake in a 350° oven 15 minutes. Add 1 minced clove garlic and bake uncovered 20 minutes longer or until hot and tender, basting frequently. Arrange 1 cup sautéed pineapple chunks around the duck.

Serves 4 each time.

DUCK, SPANISH STYLE

3 5-pound ducks, disjointed
4 teaspoons salt
¾ teaspoon freshly ground black pepper
2 teaspoons paprika
½ cup flour
2 tablespoons olive oil
2 cups dry sherry
2 cups fresh or canned chicken broth
2 bay leaves
¾ teaspoon thyme
1 cup sliced stuffed olives
1 cup cooked or canned tiny green peas

Wash the duck, remove as much fat as possible, and dry. Toss in a mixture of the salt, pepper, paprika, and flour.

Heat the oil in a Dutch oven or roasting pan. Brown the duck in it very well; pour off the fat. Add the sherry, broth, bay leaves, and thyme. Roast in a 350° oven 1 hour, turning the pieces and basting frequently. Transfer 2 ducks and two thirds of the gravy to a bowl or saucepan. Place in cold water or over ice to cool quickly. Skim the fat; pack into 2 containers. Seal, label, and freeze.

FOR TONIGHT'S DINNER

Add the olives and peas to the remaining duck; roast 20 minutes longer, or until tender.

TO SERVE FROM FROZEN STATE

Turn contents of one container into a casserole, cover, and bake in a 300° oven 25 minutes. Remove cover and increase heat to 350°. Add 1 cup sliced stuffed olives and 1 cup cooked or canned peas. Bake 20 minutes longer, or until hot and tender.

Serves 4 each time.

MEAT

Meat, the most expensive of all foods, should be treated with respect, so follow instructions carefully for perfect results.

Cooked roast beef, pork, lamb, ham, etc. may be frozen on the bone. Trim the fat to hinder rancidity. Wrap carefully in moisture-vaporproof wrap, label, and freeze. To serve cold, thaw while wrapped for 3–5 hours at room temperature. To serve hot, bake unwrapped in foil in a 350° oven for 30 minutes to 1 hour. Keep up to 3 months.

Sliced roast meats are best frozen when covered with gravy or sauce in a sealed container. The food may be heated while in the container (if aluminum foil is used) or cook in a double boiler until hot. Store no longer than 3 months.

Stews and pot roasts: stews should be cooked approximately 30 minutes less than the recipe specifies. Don't add potatoes, rice, or macaroni until ready to reheat. Be sure the sauce is very smooth before freezing. Chill the dish quickly by placing pot in cold water, over ice, or in the refrigerator to stop the cooking process. Skim fat, as fat turns rancid comparatively quickly. Pack in convenient-sized containers; seal, label, and freeze. Reheat in the same container (if aluminum foil or ovenproof) or turn out into a double boiler or saucepan until hot. Taste for seasoning. Store not longer than 3 months.

Meat loaf may be frozen in the loaf pan or wrapped in moisture-vaporproof wrap. Cool before wrapping. To serve cold, let thaw about 6 hours in the refrigerator. To serve hot, keep wrapped in foil and reheat frozen meat loaf in a 425° oven for 30 minutes. If preferred, the meat loaf may be sliced before freezing and frozen in individual servings for snacks or sandwiches. Keep up to 3 months.

Meat balls can be made according to your favorite recipe and frozen with the gravy. With Swedish-style meat balls (creamed), don't add the cream until ready to reheat. Pack into airtight freezer containers. To reheat, turn frozen meat balls into a skillet or saucepan and cook over low heat about 20 minutes. Store up to 2 months.

Beef pies may be prepared in large or individual-sized pie plates. Be sure the filling is cold before covering with piecrust. Seal the edges carefully and wrap in moisture- vaporproof freezer wrap and freeze. To serve, bake in a 425° oven for 50 minutes for large pies, 30 minutes for small. Keep up to 3 months.

BEEF AND HAM ROLLS

24 slices steak, about 2 by 5 inches, ¼ inch thick
24 thin slices prosciutto ham
1½ teaspoons oregano
2½ teaspoons salt
1 teaspoon pepper
½ cup olive or salad oil
4 onions, diced
4 carrots, sliced
1 pound mushrooms, sliced
1 29-ounce can Italian-style tomatoes
1 clove garlic, minced

Have the steak pounded as thin as possible, or do it yourself by placing it between 2 pieces of waxed paper and pounding with a mallet or flat side of a knife.

Place a slice of ham on each piece of steak and sprinkle with a little oregano. Roll up carefully and tie the ends with white thread or string. Sprinkle with the salt and pepper.

Heat the oil in a deep skillet; brown the rolls on all sides. Add the onions, carrots, and mushrooms; let brown. Stir in the tomatoes, cover, and cook 1 hour. Remove 12 rolls and half the sauce. Chill and pack in a freezer container; seal, label, and freeze.

FOR TONIGHT'S DINNER
Add the garlic to the remaining rolls and cook 30 minutes longer. Taste for seasoning.

TO SERVE FROM FROZEN STATE
Turn contents of the container into a saucepan. Add 1 minced clove garlic; cover and cook over low heat 30 minutes, or until very hot and tender.

Serves 6 each time.

BOEUF BOURGUIGNONNE

½ cup flour
2½ teaspoons salt
¾ teaspoon pepper
6 pounds beef (chuck, top or bottom round)
    cut in 1½-inch cubes
½ cup butter or oil
1 slice salt pork, diced
4 onions, diced
2 carrots, sliced
2 bay leaves
4 cups dry red wine
3 tablespoons chopped parsley
¼ teaspoon thyme
¼ pound mushrooms, sliced

Mix the flour, salt, and pepper together; roll the meat in it.

Melt the butter in a Dutch oven, heavy saucepan, or heatproof casserole and brown the meat in it on all sides.

Brown the salt pork in a skillet; pour off most of the fat. Add the onions and carrots; sauté until browned. Add to the beef with the bay leaves, wine, and parsley. Cover and cook over low heat 2 hours. Transfer half the mixture to a bowl; place in cold water or over ice to cool quickly. Pack in a container; seal, label, and freeze.

FOR TONIGHT'S DINNER

To the remaining beef, add the thyme and mushrooms. Cover and cook over low heat 1 hour longer or until meat is very tender. Taste for seasoning.

TO SERVE FROM FROZEN STATE

Turn into a saucepan. Add ¼ teaspoon thyme and ¼ pound sliced mushrooms. Cover and cook over low heat 1 hour. Taste for seasoning.

Serves 6–8 each time.

BOEUF À LA FLAMANDE

6 pounds beef (top round, eye round)
4 tablespoons butter
3 cups sliced onions
3 tablespoons flour
2½ teaspoons salt
¾ teaspoon pepper
3 cups beer
2 tablespoons vinegar
2 teaspoons sugar
3 tablespoons chopped parsley
2 bay leaves
¼ teaspoon thyme

Have the beef cut 1 inch thick and then into about 18 pieces. Melt the butter in a Dutch oven or heavy skillet; sauté the onions until brown, stirring frequently. Remove the onions. Brown the beef in the fat remaining in the pan. Sprinkle with the flour, salt, and pepper. Add the beer, vinegar, sugar, parsley, bay leaves, and sautéed onions. Mix well. Cover and cook over low heat 1½ hours. Transfer half the meat and gravy to a bowl; place in cold water to chill rapidly. Pack in a container; seal, label, and freeze.

FOR TONIGHT'S DINNER
Add the thyme to the remaining meat and cook 30 minutes longer, or until tender.

TO SERVE FROM FROZEN STATE
Turn into a saucepan; add ¼ teaspoon thyme, cover, and cook over low heat 40 minutes or until hot and tender.
Serves 6 each time.

BEEF STROGANOFF

3 pounds fillet of beef
2½ teaspoons salt
½ teaspoon freshly ground black pepper
⅜ pound (¾ cup) butter
3 tablespoons flour
2½ cups beef broth
1 cup thinly sliced onions
1 pound mushrooms, thinly sliced
4 tablespoons sour cream

Slice the beef ½ inch thick and into ½-inch-wide strips. Toss with the salt and pepper.

Melt 4 tablespoons butter in a saucepan; stir in the flour until golden, then gradually add the broth, stirring steadily to the boiling point. Cook over low heat 5 minutes.

Melt 4 tablespoons butter in a skillet; brown the meat in it. Add to the sauce and cook over low heat 5 minutes. Melt the remaining butter in the skillet; sauté the onions and mushrooms 5 minutes. Mix into the meat. Transfer half the mixture to a bowl; place in cold water or over ice to cool quickly. Pack into a container; seal, label, and freeze.

FOR TONIGHT'S DINNER

Cover the remaining beef; cook over low heat 15 minutes. Stir in the sour cream, heat, and taste for seasoning.

TO SERVE FROM FROZEN STATE

Turn into a saucepan, cover, and cook over low heat until thawed; then cook 10 minutes longer. Stir in 4 tablespoons sour cream, heat, and taste for seasoning.

Serves 4–6 each time.

GYPSY RAGOUT

6 pounds top sirloin
4 tablespoons salad oil
5 cups thinly sliced onions
2½ teaspoons salt
3 tablespoons flour
3 tablespoons paprika
4 cups dry red wine
1½ cups sour cream

Have the meat cut ¼ inch thick and into strips 3 inches long by ¼ inch wide.

Heat the oil in a Dutch oven or casserole; brown the meat and onions in it. Sprinkle with the salt, flour, and paprika, then gradually add the wine. Bring to a boil, stirring lightly. Cover and bake in a 375° oven 1 hour. Transfer two thirds of the mixture to a bowl or saucepan; place in cold water or over ice to cool quickly. Pack into 2 containers; seal, label, and freeze.

FOR TONIGHT'S DINNER

Stir half the sour cream into the remaining meat and gravy. Bake 30 minutes longer. Blend in the remaining sour cream; heat over direct low heat but do not let boil. Taste for seasoning.

TO SERVE FROM FROZEN STATE

Turn contents of one container into a casserole; cover and bake in a 325° oven 20 minutes. Stir in ¾ cup sour cream; re-cover and bake 30 minutes, or until meat is very hot and tender. Place over direct low heat and stir in ¾ cup sour cream. Heat, but do not let boil. Taste for seasoning.

Serves 4–6 each time.

FRENCH POT ROAST

9 pounds eye round
4 cups dry red wine
2 tablespoons wine vinegar
1 tablespoon salt
¾ teaspoon freshly ground black pepper
2 bay leaves
½ teaspoon rosemary
¼ teaspoon nutmeg
2 onions, thinly sliced
3 tablespoons oil
1 veal knuckle
1 clove garlic, minced
2 tablespoons cognac
12 small white onions
4 carrots, quartered
12 mushroom caps

Have the meat larded and cut in three 3-pound pieces. In a bowl (not metal) combine the wine, vinegar, salt, pepper, bay leaves, rosemary, nutmeg, and sliced onions. Marinate the meat in the refrigerator for 24 hours. Drain, dry, and reserve marinade.

Heat the oil in a Dutch oven or heavy saucepan; brown the meat in it. Pour off the fat. Heat the marinade and add with the veal knuckle. Cover and roast in a 350° oven 3 hours. Transfer 2 pieces of meat and two thirds of the gravy to a bowl or saucepan. Place in cold water or over ice to cool quickly. Slice the meat. Pack, covered with gravy, in 2 containers. Seal, label, and freeze.

FOR TONIGHT'S DINNER

To the remaining meat, add the garlic, cognac, white onions, carrots, and mushrooms. Re-cover and roast 1 hour longer. Taste for seasoning.

TO SERVE FROM FROZEN STATE

Turn contents of one container into a baking dish. Place in a 300° oven until gravy thaws. Add 1 minced clove garlic, 2 tablespoons cognac, 12 small white onions, 4 quartered carrots, and 12 mushroom caps. Re-cover and bake 45 minutes. Taste for seasoning.

Serves 6–8 each time.

HUNGARIAN GOULASH

8 pounds cross-rib or chuck
6 tablespoons butter
5 cups diced onions
1 tablespoon salt
¾ teaspoon freshly ground black pepper
4 tablespoons Hungarian paprika
2 8-ounce cans tomato sauce
½ cup sour cream

Cut the beef in 1½-inch cubes. Melt the butter in a Dutch oven or heavy saucepan; sauté the onions over low heat until soft and transparent. Add the meat and brown over high heat. Stir in the salt, pepper, and paprika until meat is well coated. Mix in the tomato sauce; cover tightly and cook over low heat 1½ hours.

Transfer two thirds of the mixture to a bowl or saucepan and place in cold water or over ice to cool quickly. Pack into two containers; seal, label, and freeze.

FOR TONIGHT'S DINNER
Continue cooking remaining goulash 30 minutes longer. Stir in the sour cream; heat, but do not let boil.

TO SERVE FROM FROZEN STATE
Turn contents of one container into a heavy saucepan, cover, and cook over very low heat until mixture thaws, then cook over low heat 20 minutes. Stir in ½ cup sour cream; heat, but do not let boil. Taste for seasoning and serve.

Serves 4–5 each time.

BEEF RAGOUT

8 pounds cross-rib or bottom round
2 cups dry red wine
1 tablespoon salt
¾ teaspoon freshly ground black pepper
2 bay leaves
4 cloves
½ teaspoon thyme
¼ cup olive oil
3 cups fresh or canned beef broth
4 sprigs parsley
24 small white onions
24 mushroom caps
8 carrots, sliced
1 clove garlic, minced, or ¼ teaspoon garlic powder
1 cup cooked or canned green peas

Cut the beef in 2-inch pieces. Combine the wine, salt, pepper, bay leaves, cloves, and thyme in a bowl (not metal). Marinate the meat in the mixture overnight. Drain, reserving the marinade.

Heat the oil in a Dutch oven or casserole; brown the meat in it over high heat. Stir in the broth, parsley, and reserved marinade. Bring to a boil and cook over high heat 20 minutes. Cover, reduce heat to low, and cook 1 hour. Add the onions, mushrooms, and carrots. Re-cover and cook 30 minutes. Transfer two thirds of the mixture to a bowl or saucepan and place in cold water or over ice to cool quickly. Pack into 2 containers; seal, label, and freeze.

FOR TONIGHT'S DINNER

Add the garlic to the remaining mixture and cook 30 minutes longer. Add the peas. Heat, taste for seasoning, and serve.

TO SERVE FROM FROZEN STATE

Turn contents of one container into a heavy pan, add 1 clove minced garlic, and cook over low heat 20 minutes after the mixture thaws. Stir in 1 cup cooked or canned peas, season, and serve. Serves 4–5 each time.

SWEET AND SOUR CHINESE MEAT BALLS

½ cup salad oil
1½ cups thinly sliced onions
4 tablespoons honey
⅓ cup sugar
⅔ cup vinegar
1½ teaspoons powdered ginger
3 tablespoons cornstarch
2 tablespoons soy sauce
2 cups water
3 pounds ground beef
1½ teaspoons salt
½ teaspoon freshly ground black pepper
2 eggs, beaten
2 tomatoes, diced

Heat ⅓ cup oil in a saucepan; sauté the onions 5 minutes. Mix in the honey, sugar, vinegar, and ginger; cook over low heat 5 minutes. Mix the cornstarch until smooth with the soy sauce and 1½ cups water; add to the previous mixture, stirring steadily until thickened.

Mix the beef, salt, pepper, eggs, and remaining water together; shape into 1-inch balls. Heat the remaining oil in a skillet; brown the balls in it, shaking the pan to keep the balls round. Drain and divide balls and sauce into 2 equal quantities. Place one bowl in cold water or over ice to cool quickly. Pack into a container; seal, label, and freeze.

FOR TONIGHT'S DINNER
Cook the remaining meat balls for 5 minutes. Add tomatoes and cook 5 minutes longer.

TO SERVE FROM FROZEN STATE
Turn into a saucepan; cover and cook over low heat until thawed. Add 2 diced tomatoes; cook 5 minutes, or until very hot.
Serves 4–6 each time.

SWEDISH MEAT BALLS

2 cups chopped onions
¼ pound butter
2 cups dry bread crumbs
1½ cups light cream
2 pounds ground beef
1 pound ground pork
1 pound ground veal
2½ teaspoons salt
¾ teaspoon white pepper
½ teaspoon nutmeg
4 eggs, beaten
3 tablespoons minced parsley
3 tablespoons flour
3 cups heavy cream

Brown the onions in 3 tablespoons butter. Soak the bread crumbs in the light cream 10 minutes.

Lightly mix together the beef, pork, veal, salt, pepper, nutmeg, eggs, parsley, sautéed onions, and undrained bread crumbs. Shape into 1-inch balls.

Melt the remaining butter in a skillet; brown the balls in it on all sides, shaking the pan frequently. Remove meat balls. Blend the flour into the butter remaining in the skillet. Gradually add the heavy cream, stirring steadily to the boiling point. Cook over low heat 5 minutes. Taste for seasoning

Divide the meat balls into 3 equal amounts. Pack 2 parts into individual containers and cover with sauce. Cool, seal, label, and freeze.

FOR TONIGHT'S DINNER

Cook the remaining meat balls in the remaining sauce over low heat for 15 minutes.

TO SERVE FROM FROZEN STATE

Turn contents of one container into the top of a double boiler.

Cover, place over hot water, and cook until mixture thaws. Uncover and cook 15 minutes. Taste for seasoning.

Serves 3–4 each time. Smaller-sized meat balls make excellent hot hors d'oeuvres.

MEAT LOAF

3 pounds ground beef
¾ cup finely chopped onions
¼ cup finely chopped green peppers
3 teaspoons salt
¼ teaspoon freshly ground black pepper
1 teaspoon dry mustard
2 cups soft bread crumbs
3 eggs, lightly beaten
3 cups condensed tomato soup
4 tablespoons butter

Mix together lightly all the ingredients but the butter. Shape into 2 loaves.

Melt the butter in a shallow pan and place the loaves in it. Bake in a 400° oven for 35 minutes, basting occasionally. Transfer 1 loaf to a bowl; place in cold water or over ice to cool quickly. Wrap, seal, label, and freeze.

FOR TONIGHT'S DINNER
Continue baking the remaining loaf 15 minutes. Slice and serve.

TO SERVE FROM FROZEN STATE
Unwrap and place on a buttered baking pan. Bake in a 375° oven 45 minutes, or until very hot. Slice and serve.

Serves 4–6 each time.

Note: If you intend to serve the loaf cold, bake it 50 minutes before freezing. The loaf may be sliced before freezing.

SAUERBRATEN

3 cups cider vinegar
1½ cups water
12 peppercorns
6 cloves
4 bay leaves
1 tablespoon salt
2 onions, sliced
8 pounds eye or bottom round
3 tablespoons beef fat or oil
2 cups chopped onions
2 cups grated carrots
¼ cup sugar
1 clove garlic, minced
½ cup sour cream

In a saucepan, bring to a boil the vinegar, water, peppercorns, cloves, bay leaves, salt, and sliced onions. Cut meat in thirds crosswise and place in a bowl (not metal); pour the hot vinegar mixture over it. Cool, and marinate in the refrigerator 2–3 days, turning the meat a few times. Drain and dry the meat; reserve 3 cups marinade.

Heat the oil in a Dutch oven or heavy saucepan; brown the meat in it. Add the onions and let brown. Mix in the carrots, sugar, and marinade. Cover tightly and cook over low heat 2½ hours. Transfer 2 pieces of meat and two thirds of the gravy to a bowl or saucepan. Place in cold water or over ice to cool quickly. Slice the meat and pack into 2 containers with the gravy. Seal, label, and freeze.

FOR TONIGHT'S DINNER
Add the garlic to the remaining meat; re-cover and cook 30 minutes longer. Stir in the sour cream and taste for seasoning; heat but do not let boil.

TO SERVE FROM FROZEN STATE
Turn contents of one container into a heavy saucepan; cover and

cook over very low heat until mixture thaws. Stir in 1 clove minced garlic, re-cover, and cook over low heat 20 minutes. Blend in ½ cup sour cream; taste for seasoning, heat, but do not let boil.

Serves 4–5 each time.

HAMBURGERS

2 pounds ground beef
2 teaspoons salt
¼ teaspoon freshly ground black pepper
½ teaspoon Ac'cent
4 tablespoons grated onions
2 tablespoons butter

Mix together all the ingredients but the butter. Shape into 8 patties. Wrap 4; seal, label, and freeze.

FOR TONIGHT'S DINNER

Melt the butter in a skillet. Cook the patties in it over high heat 4–8 minutes, depending on how you like them. Turn patties once.

TO SERVE FROM FROZEN STATE

Remove patties from freezer 1 hour before needed. Keep wrapped until ready to cook. Melt 2 tablespoons butter in a skillet and cook the patties 4–8 minutes.

Serves 4 each time.

STUFFED PEPPERS

18 green peppers
2½ pounds ground beef
½ cup raw rice
2 eggs
½ teaspoon freshly ground black pepper
4 teaspoons salt
1 10¾-ounce can condensed tomato soup
2 tablespoons butter
1 cup diced onions
1 29-ounce can tomatoes, drained
1 8-ounce can tomato sauce
1 beef bone
4 tablespoons lemon juice
⅓ cup sugar

Buy uniform, large-sized peppers. Wash, drain, and cut a 1-inch piece from the stem end. Scoop out the seeds and fibers. Reserve the tops. Mix together the beef, rice, eggs, black pepper, 2 teaspoons salt, and the tomato soup. Stuff the peppers and place the tops on them.

Melt the butter in a Dutch oven or casserole. Sauté the onions 10 minutes. Add the tomatoes, tomato sauce, bone, and remaining salt. Bring to a boil and arrange the peppers in it. Cover loosely and cook over low heat 20 minutes. Stir in the lemon juice and sugar. Re-cover and cook 20 minutes. Shake the pan frequently. Transfer 12 peppers and two thirds of the sauce to a bowl or saucepan; place in cold water or over ice to cool quickly. Skim the fat. Arrange the peppers and sauce in 2 containers; seal, label, and freeze.

FOR TONIGHT'S DINNER

Cook the remaining peppers 20 minutes longer, or until tender. Taste for seasoning.

TO SERVE FROM FROZEN STATE

Turn contents of one container into a casserole or saucepan.

Cover and cook over low heat 40 minutes, or until very hot. Taste for seasoning.

Serves 4–6 each time.

BAKED STUFFED PEPPERS

12 green peppers
3 tablespoons butter
2 onions, finely chopped
1¼ pounds ground beef
2 tomatoes, peeled and chopped
1½ teaspoons salt
¼ teaspoon pepper
1½ cups canned tomato sauce
¼ teaspoon basil

Cut a 1-inch piece from the stem end of the peppers and reserve. Carefully scoop out the seeds and fibers. Parboil the peppers and the ends for 5 minutes in boiling salted water; drain and cool.

Melt the butter in a skillet; sauté the onions 5 minutes. Stir in the beef and tomatoes; cook over high heat 5 minutes, or until the beef loses its redness. Add the salt and pepper. Mix well and taste for seasoning. Chill, then fill the peppers. Cover with reserved ends, pressing down firmly. Pack 6 peppers in a freezer container; seal, label, and freeze.

FOR TONIGHT'S DINNER

Arrange the remaining peppers in a baking dish. Add the tomato sauce and basil. Bake in a 375° oven 45 minutes, or until very hot. Taste for seasoning and serve.

TO SERVE FROM FROZEN STATE

Turn the peppers into a baking dish. Add 1½ cups canned tomato sauce and ¼ teaspoon basil. Cover and bake in a 375° oven 30 minutes. Remove cover and bake 30 minutes longer. Taste for seasoning.

Serves 6 each time.

ITALIAN HASH

3 tablespoons olive oil
1½ cups thinly sliced onions
1 cup sliced carrots
2 pounds ground beef
1 pound ground veal
1 pound ground pork
2 tablespoons flour
3 cups fresh or canned beef broth
1 tablespoon tomato paste
1½ teaspoons salt
½ teaspoon freshly ground black pepper
1 cup chopped mushrooms
3 chicken livers, chopped
½ cup heavy cream

Heat the oil in a skillet; sauté the onions and carrots 10 minutes. Add the beef, veal, and pork; cook over medium heat, stirring almost constantly, until meat browns. Add the broth, tomato paste, salt, and pepper. Stir in flour. Cover and cook over low heat 45 minutes. Transfer two thirds of the mixture to a bowl or saucepan; place in cold water or over ice to cool quickly. Pack into 2 containers; seal, label, and freeze.

FOR TONIGHT'S DINNER

To the remaining meat, add the mushrooms and livers; cover and cook over low heat 25 minutes. Just before serving, mix in the cream. Taste for seasoning.

TO SERVE FROM FROZEN STATE

Turn contents of one container into a saucepan; cover and cook over low heat 20 minutes. Add 1 cup chopped mushrooms and 3 chopped chicken livers. Re-cover and cook 20 minutes, or until very hot. Just before serving, mix in ½ cup heavy cream. Taste for seasoning.

Serves 4–5 each time.

BEEF AND EGGPLANT CASSEROLE

4 pounds fillet of beef or sirloin steak
⅔ cup olive oil
2 eggplants
½ cup flour
2 cups diced onions
4 cups drained canned tomatoes
2½ teaspoons salt
½ teaspoon freshly ground black pepper
½ teaspoon basil
4 tablespoons minced parsley
⅓ cup dry bread crumbs

Slice the fillet ¼ inch thick or buy sirloin steak cut ¼ inch thick and then cut into 16 pieces. Heat 2 tablespoons oil in a skillet and brown the meat over high heat on both sides. Remove.

Peel and slice the eggplants ¼ inch thick. Dip in the flour. Heat 4 tablespoons oil in the skillet and brown the eggplant in it. Remove. Heat the remaining oil in the skillet; sauté the onions 10 minutes. Stir in the tomatoes, salt, pepper, basil, and parsley. Cook over low heat 10 minutes. Use 3 casseroles or 1 casserole and 2 aluminum-foil containers with covers. Divide equally and arrange eggplant on the bottom with the meat and sauce over it. Cover 2 containers; seal, label, and freeze.

FOR TONIGHT'S DINNER
Sprinkle the bread crumbs on the remaining casserole; bake in a 350° oven 30 minutes.

TO SERVE FROM FROZEN STATE
Place casserole or container in a 350° oven for 15 minutes. Remove cover, sprinkle with ⅓ cup bread crumbs, and bake 20 minutes longer, or until very hot.

Serves 4 each time.

BRETON LAMB AND BEANS

3 cups dried white beans
6 pounds boneless lamb
1 tablespoon salt
¾ teaspoon freshly ground black pepper
3 tablespoons butter
3 cups diced onions
3 cups diced tomatoes
¾ teaspoon thyme
2 bay leaves
3 sprigs parsley
3 cups boiling water
2 cloves garlic, minced

Wash the beans, cover with water, bring to a boil, and let soak 1 hour. Drain. Add fresh water to cover, bring to a boil, cover, and cook 30 minutes. Drain.

Cut the lamb in 2-inch pieces; season with the salt and pepper. Melt the butter in a Dutch oven or heavy saucepan; brown the meat and onions in it. Add the tomatoes, thyme, bay leaves, parsley, water, and beans. Cover and cook over low heat 1 hour. Discard bay leaves and parsley. Transfer two thirds of the mixture to a bowl or saucepan; place in cold water or over ice to cool quickly. Pack into 2 containers; seal, label, and freeze.

FOR TONIGHT'S DINNER

Add the garlic to the remaining lamb; re-cover and cook 30 minutes longer, or until meat and beans are tender. Watch carefully and add a little boiling water if necessary. Taste for seasoning.

TO SERVE FROM FROZEN STATE

Turn contents of one container into a casserole, cover, and place in a 350° oven until thawed (about 20 minutes). Add 2 minced cloves garlic, re-cover, and bake 30 minutes longer or until very hot. Watch carefully and add a little boiling water if necessary.

Serves 4–6 each time.

LAMB RAGOUT

6 pounds boneless lamb
2½ teaspoons salt
¾ teaspoon freshly ground black pepper
⅛ teaspoon ground allspice
4 tablespoons olive oil
½ pound ham, diced
2 cups chopped onions
2 cups fresh or canned beef broth
½ cup dry red wine
2 bay leaves
1½ cups diced potatoes
2 cups shelled green peas or 1 package frozen, thawed

Cut the lamb in 1½-inch cubes; toss with the salt, pepper, and allspice.

Heat the oil in a heavy saucepan or Dutch oven, brown the lamb and ham in it. Add the onions and let brown. Stir in the broth, wine, and bay leaves. Cover and cook over low heat 1 hour.

Transfer two thirds of the mixture to a bowl or saucepan. Place in cold water or over ice to cool quickly. Pack into 2 containers; seal, label, and freeze.

FOR TONIGHT'S DINNER

Add the potatoes and peas to the remaining lamb; re-cover and cook over low heat 20 minutes, or until lamb and potatoes are tender. Taste for seasoning.

TO SERVE FROM FROZEN STATE

Turn contents of one container into a heavy saucepan, cover, and cook over low heat until gravy thaws. Add 1½ cups diced potatoes and 2 cups shelled green peas (fresh or frozen). Re-cover and cook 20 minutes. Taste for seasoning.

Serves 4–5 each time.

PORK IN RED WINE

4 cups dry red wine
1 tablespoon wine vinegar
1½ cups chopped onions
1 tablespoon salt
¾ teaspoon freshly ground black pepper
½ teaspoon marjoram
2 bay leaves
8 pounds boned loin of pork
2 tablespoons butter
¼ cup currant jelly

Bring the wine, vinegar, onions, salt, pepper, marjoram, and bay leaves to a boil. Cut the pork in 3 equal pieces and place in a bowl (not metal). Pour the hot marinade over it. Marinate in the refrigerator 24 hours, turning the meat a few times. Drain and dry the meat; heat the marinade.

Heat the butter in a Dutch oven or heavy saucepan; brown the meat in it. Pour off the fat. Add the hot marinade; cover and roast in a 350° oven 2 hours. Transfer 2 pieces of pork and two thirds the marinade to a bowl or saucepan. Place in cold water or over ice to cool quickly. Skim the fat and slice the meat. Pack in 2 containers; seal, label, and freeze.

FOR TONIGHT'S DINNER

Continue roasting the remaining pork, uncovered, for 30 minutes. Skim the fat, place over direct heat, and stir the jelly into the gravy. Taste for seasoning.

TO SERVE FROM FROZEN STATE

Turn contents of one container into a casserole or skillet and place, covered, in a 350° oven until gravy thaws. Remove cover and bake 20 minutes, or until very hot. Place over direct heat, stir ¼ cup currant jelly into the gravy; taste for seasoning.

Serves 4 each time.

LOIN OF PORK IN ORANGE SAUCE

2 5-pound loins of pork
2 teaspoons salt
½ teaspoon freshly ground black pepper
½ teaspoon oregano
1 cup thinly sliced onions
4 cups orange juice
3 tablespoons wine vinegar
2 tablespoons currant jelly
2 oranges, peeled and segmented

Rub the pork with the salt, pepper, and oregano. Place in a shallow roasting pan, fat side up. Roast in a 425° oven 30 minutes. Pour off the fat. Add the onions and orange juice mixed with the vinegar. Reduce heat to 350° and roast 1½ hours, basting frequently. Transfer 1 loin and half the gravy to a bowl or saucepan; place in cold water or over ice to cool quickly. Skim the fat, slice the pork. Pack into a container with the gravy covering the pork. Seal, label, and freeze.

FOR TONIGHT'S DINNER
Stir the jelly into the gravy remaining in the pan and arrange the oranges around the pork. Roast 30 minutes longer, basting frequently. Transfer the pork and oranges to a platter and strain the skimmed gravy into a sauceboat.

TO SERVE FROM FROZEN STATE
Turn into a skillet or shallow casserole, cover, and bake in a 300° oven 20 minutes. Stir 2 tablespoons currant jelly into the gravy and arrange 2 peeled and segmented oranges on top. Bake uncovered 30 minutes, basting frequently.
Serves 4–6 each time.

MARINATED SPARERIBS

4 racks of spareribs
2½ teaspoons salt
¾ teaspoon freshly ground black pepper
1 tablespoon paprika
1 cup sweet sherry
2 tablespoons lemon juice
2 tablespoons salad oil
2 cups chopped onions
2 cloves garlic, minced
2 cups drained canned tomatoes
1½ cups wine vinegar
1 teaspoon dry mustard
3 tablespoons Worcestershire sauce
2 tablespoons chili powder
¼ teaspoon Tabasco
3 tablespoons sugar
1 teaspoon thyme

Have the ribs cut in serving-sized pieces. Rub with the salt, pepper, and paprika. Place in a bowl (not metal) and add the sherry, mixed with the lemon juice. Marinate in the refrigerator 4 hours or overnight, turning and basting the ribs a few times.

Heat the oil in a saucepan; sauté the onions and garlic 10 minutes. Add the tomatoes, vinegar, mustard, Worcestershire sauce, chili powder, Tabasco, sugar, and thyme. Cook over low heat 10 minutes. Drain the ribs and arrange in a shallow pan. Brush with tomato sauce. Bake in a 350° oven 45 minutes, basting frequently. Remove half the ribs and gravy. Add half the remaining sauce. Cool quickly; skim fat. Pack in container; seal, label, and freeze.

FOR TONIGHT'S DINNER
Continue baking the ribs 30 minutes longer, basting frequently with remaining sauce.

TO SERVE FROM FROZEN STATE
Turn into a shallow pan; cover with aluminum foil. Bake in a

300° oven 20 minutes. Remove foil and separate ribs; bake 30 minutes longer, basting frequently.

Serves 4–6 each time.

CHILI CON CARNE

3 cups dried red beans or 6 cups canned
⅓ cup salad oil
1½ cups chopped onions
4 pounds lean beef, cut in ¼-inch cubes
4 teaspoons chili powder
3 tablespoons flour
2 29-ounce cans tomatoes
1 tablespoon salt
2 cloves garlic, minced

If dried beans are used, wash carefully and soak overnight in water to cover. Drain. Cover with fresh water and cook over medium heat 1 hour. Drain.

Heat the oil in a heavy saucepan. Add the onions and beef; cook over high heat, stirring almost constantly until browned. Sprinkle with the chili powder and flour. Mix well. Add the tomatoes. Cover and cook over low heat 1½ hours. Add salt and cooked or canned beans. Remove two thirds of the mixture. Chill and pack in 2 jars or freezer containers; seal, label, and freeze.

FOR TONIGHT'S DINNER

Add the garlic to the remaining chili and cook 45 minutes longer. Taste for seasoning.

TO SERVE FROM FROZEN STATE

Turn contents of one container into a saucepan and add 2 minced cloves garlic. Cover and cook over low heat 1 hour.

Serves 4–6 each time.

VEAL MARENGO

6 pounds shoulder of veal
4 tablespoons olive oil
1¼ cups chopped onions
2½ teaspoons salt
½ teaspoon freshly ground black pepper
3 tablespoons flour
3 cups diced peeled fresh or canned tomatoes
2 cups dry white wine
1½ cups fresh or canned chicken broth
1 clove garlic, minced
1 cup sliced mushrooms
2 tablespoons butter

Cut the veal in 1½-inch cubes. Heat the oil in a casserole or heavy saucepan; brown the veal in it. Add the onions and continue browning. Sprinkle with the salt, pepper, and flour. Mix in the tomatoes, wine, and broth. Cover and cook over low heat 1 hour.

Transfer two thirds of the mixture to a bowl or saucepan and place in cold water or over ice to cool quickly. Pack into 2 containers; seal, label, and freeze.

FOR TONIGHT'S DINNER

Sauté the garlic and mushrooms in the butter for 3 minutes. Add to the remaining veal. Re-cover and cook over low heat 15 minutes, or until tender. Taste for seasoning and serve with sautéed French bread.

TO SERVE FROM FROZEN STATE

Turn the contents of one container into a heavy saucepan. Cover and cook over very low heat until thawed. Add 1 minced clove garlic and 1 cup sliced mushrooms, sautéed in 2 tablespoons butter. Re-cover and cook over low heat 15 minutes. Taste for seasoning.

Serves 4–6 each time.

VEAL AND MUSHROOMS

24 scallops of veal
1 tablespoon salt
½ teaspoon white pepper
¼ pound butter
2 cups diced onions
3 tablespoons flour
1½ cups fresh or canned chicken broth
1½ cups light cream
4 egg yolks
1 pound mushrooms, sliced

Season the veal with half the salt and pepper. Melt 3 tablespoons butter in a saucepan; cook the onions over low heat until transparent and yellow but not brown. Blend in the flour, then gradually add the broth, cream, and remaining salt and pepper, stirring steadily to the boiling point. Cover and cook over low heat 20 minutes. Purée in an electric blender or force through a sieve. Beat the egg yolks in a bowl; gradually add the hot sauce, stirring steadily to prevent curdling. Return to the saucepan and cook over low heat, stirring steadily until thickened. Do not let boil.

Melt half the remaining butter in a skillet; sauté mushrooms 5 minutes. Add remaining butter to skillet; brown veal in it.

Arrange 8 slices of veal in 3 casseroles or 1 casserole and 2 freezer containers, with the mushrooms around them and sauce over all. Chill 2 casseroles or containers; seal, label, and freeze.

FOR TONIGHT'S DINNER
Bake the remaining casserole in a 450° oven 15 minutes.

TO SERVE FROM FROZEN STATE
If ovenproof casseroles or containers were used, place one directly in a 400° oven, covered, for 10 minutes. Remove cover, raise heat to 450°, and bake 10 minutes or until delicately browned and hot. If not frozen in an ovenproof dish, turn mixture into one and follow instructions for baking.
Serves 4 each time.

CASSEROLE OF VEAL BIRDS

4 pounds leg of veal
2½ teaspoons salt
½ teaspoon white pepper
½ teaspoon nutmeg
½ teaspoon thyme
½ pound sausage meat
½ teaspoon basil
4 tablespoons grated onions
4 tablespoons minced parsley
½ teaspoon freshly ground black pepper
6 tablespoons butter
1½ cups dry white wine
12 small white onions
1 pound mushrooms, sliced
2 bay leaves

Have the butcher cut the veal ¼ inch thick and pound it as thin as possible. Cut into 12 pieces about 3 × 6 inches each. Rub with a mixture of the salt, white pepper, nutmeg, and thyme.

Mix together the sausage meat, basil, onions, parsley, and black pepper. Place 1 tablespoon of the mixture on each piece of veal. Roll up and tie with white thread.

Melt the butter in a casserole or deep skillet; brown the veal rolls in it on all sides. Add the wine, white onions, mushrooms, and bay leaves. Cover and bake in a 375° oven 30 minutes. Shake skillet frequently.

Transfer 8 rolls and two thirds the gravy and vegetables to a bowl or saucepan. Place in cold water or over ice to cool quickly. Pack into 2 containers; seal, label, and freeze.

FOR TONIGHT'S DINNER

Continue baking the remaining rolls 20 minutes, or until tender. Taste for seasoning.

TO SERVE FROM FROZEN STATE

Turn into a casserole, cover, and bake in a 350° oven 35 minutes, or until very hot. Taste for seasoning.

Serves 4 each time.

VEAL CACCIATORA

4 pounds leg of veal
½ cup flour
3 teaspoons salt
¾ teaspoon freshly ground black pepper
4 tablespoons olive oil
1 cup chopped onions
½ pound mushrooms, sliced
¾ cup dry white wine
2½ cups drained canned tomatoes
¾ teaspoon basil
4 tablespoons butter
1 tablespoon minced parsley

Have the veal cut ¼ inch thick, then pounded as thin as possible. Cut into 24 scallops (or ask for 24 scallops). Mix the flour with half the salt and pepper; dip the veal in it lightly.

Heat the oil in a saucepan; sauté the onions and mushrooms 10 minutes. Add the wine; cook over high heat 5 minutes. Stir in the tomatoes, basil, and remaining salt and pepper.

While the sauce is cooking, prepare the veal. Melt the butter in a skillet; sauté the veal until browned and tender. Remove the veal. Stir the sauce into the skillet, scraping up the browned particles. Taste for seasoning.

Pack 8 scallops in each of 2 containers. Cover with some sauce; chill, seal, label, and freeze.

FOR TONIGHT'S DINNER
Return the remaining scallops to the sauce remaining in the skillet; sprinkle with the parsley, heat, and serve.

TO SERVE FROM THE FROZEN STATE
If heatproof container was used, place in a 350° oven for 20 minutes or until hot. Remove cover for last 5 minutes, or turn into covered skillet and heat as directed. Sprinkle with 1 tablespoon minced parsley before serving.

Serves 4 each time.

OSSO BUCO

6 pounds veal shank bones
½ cup flour
1 tablespoon salt
½ teaspoon freshly ground black pepper
4 tablespoons olive oil
2 cups chopped onions
3 cups fresh or canned beef broth
2 cups dry red wine
2 cups peeled chopped tomatoes
1 teaspoon basil
4 tablespoons minced parsley
1 clove garlic, minced

Have the bones cut in 3-inch pieces; roll lightly in a mixture of the flour, salt, and pepper. Heat the oil in a Dutch oven or heavy saucepan; brown the shanks and onions in it very well. Add the broth, wine, tomatoes, basil, and parsley. Bring to a boil, cover, and cook over low heat 2 hours. Transfer half the shanks and gravy to a bowl or saucepan; place in cold water or over ice to cool quickly. Pack into a container; seal, label, and freeze.

FOR TONIGHT'S DINNER

Add the garlic to remaining shanks; re-cover and cook 30 minutes, or until tender. Taste for seasoning. Serve with risotto (see recipe).

TO SERVE FROM FROZEN STATE

Turn into a Dutch oven or heavy saucepan; add 1 minced clove garlic. Cover and cook over low heat 1 hour, or until tender and very hot. Mix occasionally. Taste for seasoning.

Serves 4–6 each time.

VEGETABLES AND PASTAS

Most vegetables cook quickly, so don't freeze plain boiled or steamed ones. However, unusual vegetable dishes are tempting to your family and guests, so prepare them in large quantities and freeze them for future use. In just a few minutes you will have a delicious, novel vegetable course.

White and sweet potatoes may be frozen when cooked, stuffed, candied, or in pancake form. Pack into freezer containers, and reheat in a covered baking dish, saucepan, or double boiler.

CARROT PUDDING

24 carrots
6 tablespoons butter
¼ cup grated onions
½ cup minced green peppers
2 tablespoons flour
2 tablespoons sugar
1 teaspoon salt
¼ teaspoon white pepper
¼ teaspoon mace
2 cups milk
¼ cup dry bread crumbs

Pare and slice the carrots; cook in lightly salted water until tender. Drain and purée in an electric blender, or mash smooth.

Melt 4 tablespoons butter in a skillet; sauté the onions and green peppers 10 minutes but do not let brown. Blend in the flour, sugar, salt, pepper, and mace; gradually add the milk, stirring steadily to the boiling point. Cook over low heat 5 minutes. Mix with the carrots. Turn half the mixture into a casserole or bowl; place in refrigerator to cool quickly. You can freeze the pudding and remove it from the casserole or bowl, then wrap the frozen pudding in foil or freezer paper. Seal and place in the freezer again. Or wrap the casserole, seal, label, and freeze.

FOR TONIGHT'S DINNER
Put the remaining carrot mixture in a buttered casserole, sprinkle with the bread crumbs, and dot with the remaining butter. Bake in a 375° oven 30 minutes.

TO SERVE FROM FROZEN STATE
Put pudding in a buttered casserole (if it wasn't frozen in one). Place in a 325° oven for 15 minutes. Sprinkle with ¼ cup dry bread crumbs and dot with 2 tablespoons butter. Raise heat to 350° and bake 30 minutes longer, or until hot.

Serves 6–8 each time.

TURKISH EGGPLANT

4 tablespoons olive oil
1 cup chopped onions
1 cup minced parsley
1 cup chopped green peppers
6 cups diced peeled eggplant
3 tablespoons flour
2 teaspoons salt
½ teaspoon freshly ground black pepper
¾ cup hot water
2 tablespoons minced dill
¾ cup sour cream

Heat the oil in a deep skillet; sauté the onions 5 minutes. Add the parsley, green peppers, and eggplant; sauté 10 minutes, stirring frequently. Blend in the flour, salt, and pepper, then gradually add the water, stirring constantly. Cover and cook over low heat 20 minutes. Transfer half the mixture to a bowl or saucepan; place in cold water or over ice to cool quickly. Pack into a container; seal, label, and freeze.

FOR TONIGHT'S DINNER

Cook the remaining eggplant 10 minutes longer. Just before serving, mix in the dill and sour cream. Taste for seasoning.

TO SERVE FROM FROZEN STATE

Heat 1 tablespoon olive oil in a saucepan; turn in the frozen eggplant mixture. Cover and cook over low heat 25 minutes, or until very hot. Mix in 2 tablespoons minced parsley and ¾ cup sour cream. Taste for seasoning.

Serves 4–6 each time.

ITALIAN-STYLE GREEN BEANS

¼ cup olive oil
2 cups chopped onions
1 cup diced green peppers
4 cups drained canned tomatoes
2 teaspoons salt
½ teaspoon freshly ground black pepper
1 bay leaf
½ teaspoon oregano
3 pounds green beans, cut in half
1 clove garlic, minced

Heat the oil in a saucepan; sauté the onions and green peppers 10 minutes. Add the tomatoes, salt, pepper, bay leaf, and oregano. Bring to a boil and cook over low heat 20 minutes. Stir in the beans. Cover and cook over low heat 30 minutes. Transfer half the mixture to a bowl; place in cold water or over ice to cool quickly. Pack into a container; seal, label, and freeze.

FOR TONIGHT'S DINNER
Add the garlic to the remaining beans. Cover and cook 30 minutes longer. Taste for seasoning.

TO SERVE FROM FROZEN STATE
Turn into a saucepan, cover, and cook over low heat until thawed. Mix in 1 minced clove garlic, cover, and cook 20 minutes. Taste for seasoning.
Serves 6–8 each time.

SWEET AND SOUR RED CABBAGE

5 pounds red cabbage
4 tablespoons butter
2 green apples, peeled and sliced
3 tablespoons cider vinegar
4 tablespoons sugar
1½ teaspoons salt
½ cup water

Shred the cabbage very fine. Melt the butter in a large saucepan; stir in the cabbage. Cook over very low heat 5 minutes, stirring frequently. Add the apples, vinegar, sugar, salt, and water. Cover and cook over low heat 30 minutes. Watch carefully and add a little more water if necessary. Remove half the mixture and cool. Pack into a container; seal, label, and freeze.

FOR TONIGHT'S DINNER

Continue cooking the remaining cabbage 15 minutes. Taste for seasoning.

TO SERVE FROM FROZEN STATE

Turn the frozen cabbage into a saucepan. Cover and cook over low heat 40 minutes, or until very hot. Taste for seasoning.

Serves 4–6 each time.

OKRA CASSEROLE

4 pounds okra or 4 packages frozen
2 cups water
3 teaspoons salt
6 tablespoons olive oil
1½ cups chopped onions
3½ cups drained canned tomatoes
½ teaspoon freshly ground black pepper
½ teaspoon saffron
3 tablespoons dry bread crumbs

If fresh okra is used, remove the stems. Bring the water and half the salt to a boil; cook the fresh or frozen okra 4 minutes. Drain well.

Heat 4 tablespoons oil in a skillet; sauté the onions 10 minutes. Stir in the tomatoes, pepper, saffron, and remaining salt. Cover and cook over low heat 20 minutes. Lightly mix with okra. Taste for seasoning. Transfer two thirds of the mixture to a bowl or saucepan. Place in cold water or over ice to cool quickly. Pack into 2 containers; seal, label, and freeze.

FOR TONIGHT'S DINNER

Turn the remaining okra into a baking dish. Sprinkle with the bread crumbs and remaining oil. Bake in a 400° oven 15 minutes.

TO SERVE FROM FROZEN STATE

Turn contents of one container into a baking dish (if heatproof container was not used). Bake, covered, in a 350° oven 10 minutes. Remove cover, sprinkle with 3 tablespoons dry bread crumbs and 2 tablespoons olive oil, and bake 20 minutes or until hot and browned.

Serves 4 each time.

SAUTÉED SQUASH

6 pounds yellow (summer) squash or zucchini
3 tablespoons lemon juice
1 cup dry bread crumbs
¼ cup flour
6 tablespoons butter
1 teaspoon salt
¼ teaspoon pepper
2 tablespoons minced parsley

Buy young, small squash; wash, dry, and slice ¼ inch thick. Sprinkle with the lemon juice, then dip in the crumbs mixed with the flour.

Melt 3 tablespoons butter in a skillet; sauté half the slices until very lightly browned. Cool and pack in layers, with double layers of foil or freezer paper between each. Wrap, label, and freeze.

FOR TONIGHT'S DINNER

Melt the remaining butter in the skillet; sauté the remaining squash until browned on both sides and tender. Season with the salt, pepper, and parsley.

TO SERVE FROM FROZEN STATE

Melt 2 tablespoons butter in a skillet; sauté the squash until browned and tender. Season with 1 teaspoon salt, ¼ teaspoon pepper, and 2 tablespoons minced parsley.

Serves 4–6 each time.

CREAMED SPINACH

6 packages frozen spinach
4 tablespoons butter
2 tablespoons flour
1 teaspoon salt
¼ teaspoon mace
1 cup light cream

Cook the spinach as package directs. Drain well and purée in an electric blender or force through a sieve.

Melt the butter in a saucepan; blend in the flour, salt, and mace. Gradually add the cream, stirring constantly to the boiling point. Cook over low heat 5 minutes. Mix into the spinach. Remove half. Cool, pack into a container, seal, label, and freeze.

FOR TONIGHT'S DINNER
Heat the remaining spinach and taste for seasoning.

TO SERVE FROM FROZEN STATE
Turn the frozen spinach into the top of a double boiler. Place over hot water and cook, stirring frequently, until very hot. Taste for seasoning.

Serves 4–6 each time.

ZUCCHINI PROVENÇAL

5 pounds zucchini
2 tablespoons lemon juice
6 tablespoons olive oil
1 cup chopped onions
2 cups diced tomatoes
2 teaspoons salt
½ teaspoon freshly ground black pepper
½ teaspoon oregano
2 tablespoons minced parsley
1 clove garlic, minced

If very small zucchini are used, don't pare them. Otherwise pare very lightly. Toss with the lemon juice.

Heat the oil in a skillet; sauté the onions 5 minutes. Add the zucchini; sauté 5 minutes. Add the tomatoes, salt, pepper, and oregano; cover and cook over low heat 10 minutes. Transfer half the mixture to a bowl or saucepan; place in cold water or over ice to cool quickly. Pack into a container; seal, label, and freeze.

FOR TONIGHT'S DINNER

Add the parsley and garlic to the remaining zucchini; cover and cook over low heat 15 minutes. Taste for seasoning.

TO SERVE FROM FROZEN STATE

Heat 1 tablespoon olive oil in a saucepan; turn the zucchini into it. Cover and cook over low heat 10 minutes; separate the pieces. Add 2 tablespoons minced parsley and 1 minced clove garlic. Cook, uncovered, 15 minutes or until very hot. Taste for seasoning. Serves 4–6 each time.

PASTA E FAGIOLI

2 cups dried white beans
2 marrow bones
6 quarts water
⅓ cup olive oil
2 tablespoons flour
½ teaspoon rosemary
4 tablespoons minced parsley
1½ tablespoons tomato paste
1 tablespoon salt
½ teaspoon freshly ground black pepper
1 clove garlic, minced
¾ cup macaroni (short tube)

Wash the beans, cover with water, and bring to a boil. Let soak 1 hour. Drain. Combine the beans, bones, and water in a saucepan. Bring to a boil and cook over low heat 1 hour.

Heat the oil in a skillet; blend in the flour until browned. Stir in the rosemary, parsley, tomato paste, salt, and pepper. Add to the beans; cover and cook 1 hour, or until beans are tender but firm. Discard the bones, but scoop out the marrow and return to the soup. Transfer two thirds of the soup to a bowl or saucepan; place in cold water or over ice to cool quickly. Pour into 2 containers; seal, label, and freeze.

FOR TONIGHT'S DINNER

Add the garlic and macaroni to the remaining soup; cook 15 minutes or until macaroni is tender. Taste for seasoning.

TO SERVE FROM FROZEN STATE

Turn contents of one container into a saucepan; cook over low heat until thawed. Add 1 minced clove garlic and ¾ cup macaroni, half-cooked and drained. Cook over low heat 10 minutes, or until very hot and macaroni is tender. Taste for seasoning.

Serves 4–6 each time.

POTATO CROQUETTES

4 pounds potatoes
1½ teaspoons salt
¼ teaspoon white pepper
4 tablespoons butter
3 eggs
4 egg yolks
½ cup milk
2 tablespoons salad oil
¾ cup flour
1 cup dry bread crumbs
Fat for deep frying

Pare the potatoes and cut in uniform pieces. Cook in boiling salted water until tender. Drain well and shake over low heat until dry. Mash very smooth, or put through a ricer. Beat in the salt, pepper, butter, 2 eggs, and the egg yolks. Shape into 18 croquettes.

Beat the remaining egg with the milk and oil; dip the croquettes in the flour, the egg mixture and, finally, the bread crumbs. Arrange 12 croquettes on a baking sheet and freeze. Remove from the baking sheet and pack in 2 containers. (If in layers, separate with 2 layers of foil or freezer paper.) Wrap, seal, label, and freeze.

FOR TONIGHT'S DINNER
Heat the fat to 370°. Fry the remaining croquettes until browned. Drain on paper towels.

TO SERVE FROM FROZEN STATE
Heat deep fat to 360°. Fry the frozen croquettes until browned. Drain on paper towels.

Serves 6 each time.

POTATO PANCAKES

4 pounds potatoes
4 eggs, beaten
2 teaspoons salt
½ teaspoon freshly ground black pepper
4 tablespoons grated onions
4 tablespoons cracker meal
Butter, chicken fat, or oil

Pare the potatoes and grate them on the fine grater into cold water, or cut in small pieces and put in an electric blender until a smooth purée is formed. In either case, drain well. Mix in the eggs, salt, pepper, onions, and enough of the cracker meal to make a thick batter.

Heat enough of the selected fat to a depth of 1½ inches in a skillet, drop the potato mixture into it by the tablespoon. Fry two thirds of the amount until lightly browned on both sides. Drain on paper towels and cool. Arrange on a baking sheet and freeze. Pack into 2 containers with 2 sheets of foil or freezer paper between the layers. Wrap, seal, label, and freeze.

FOR TONIGHT'S DINNER

Drop the remaining batter into the hot fat by the tablespoon and fry until nicely browned on both sides. Drain on paper towels.

TO SERVE FROM FROZEN STATE

Heat the selected fat (about 1 inch deep) in a skillet. Place the frozen croquettes in it and fry until nicely browned on both sides. Drain.

Serves 4–6 each time.

BAKED STUFFED POTATOES

    6 large Idaho potatoes
    6 tablespoons butter
    1½ teaspoons salt
    ¼ teaspoon white pepper
    4 egg yolks, beaten
    ¾ cup heavy cream
    3 tablespoons dry bread crumbs

Bake the potatoes until tender. Cut in half lengthwise and scoop out the pulp; reserve the shells. Mash the pulp and beat in 5 tablespoons butter, the salt, pepper, egg yolks, and cream. Beat until smooth and light. Taste for seasoning. Pile into the shells. Freeze 6; wrap, seal, label, and return to freezer.

FOR TONIGHT'S DINNER
Sprinkle the remaining 6 halves with the bread crumbs and dot with the remaining butter. Bake in a 350° oven 10 minutes, or until browned and hot.

TO SERVE FROM FROZEN STATE
Sprinkle the frozen potatoes with 3 tablespoons bread crumbs. Dot with 2 tablespoons butter. Bake in a 325° oven 30 minutes, or until browned and hot.
Serves 6 each time.

SWEET POTATO CASSEROLE

6 pounds sweet potatoes
¾ cup butter
½ cup sweet sherry
1 cup light cream
1½ teaspoons salt
¼ teaspoon pepper
½ teaspoon cinnamon
½ teaspoon nutmeg

Boil the potatoes in their jackets about 30 minutes, or until soft. Peel and mash or put through a ricer. Add the butter, sherry, cream, salt, pepper, cinnamon, and nutmeg, mixing well.

Line a 1½-quart casserole with aluminum foil and fill with half the mixture. Chill, then freeze. Lift out the foil and overwrap the potatoes in moisture-vaporproof wrap. Return to the freezer.

FOR TONIGHT'S DINNER
Bake the remaining potatoes in a casserole in a 375° oven 30 minutes, or until delicately browned.

TO SERVE FROM FROZEN STATE
Remove from the foil and turn into the same sized casserole mixture was frozen in. Bake in a 350° oven 45 minutes, or until browned and hot.

Serves 6 each time.

CASSEROLE OF KIDNEY BEANS

4 cups kidney beans
3 quarts water
1 onion
½ cup olive oil
1½ cups chopped onions
1 cup chopped green peppers
4 cups fresh or canned chopped peeled tomatoes
2 teaspoons salt
½ teaspoon freshly ground black pepper
1 bay leaf
½ teaspoon marjoram
4 tablespoons minced parsley
1 clove garlic, minced

Wash the beans, cover with water, and bring to a boil; let soak 1 hour. Drain. Add the 3 quarts water and the onion; bring to a boil, cover, and cook over low heat 1¼ hours. Drain.

Heat the oil in a skillet; sauté the onions and green peppers 10 minutes. Stir in the tomatoes, salt, pepper, bay leaf, and marjoram. Cover and cook over low heat 20 minutes. Add to the beans. Put half the mixture in a casserole or freezer container; cool, cover, wrap, label, and freeze.

FOR TONIGHT'S DINNER

Put the remaining bean mixture in a casserole; mix in the parsley and garlic. Bake in a 350° oven 50 minutes. Taste for seasoning.

TO SERVE FROM FROZEN STATE

Turn into a casserole (if it wasn't frozen in one). Cover and place in a 300° oven for 20 minutes. Mix in ¼ cup minced parsley and 1 minced clove garlic. Raise heat to 325° and bake 40 minutes longer.

Serves 6–8 each time.

POTATO-CHEESE PIE

3 cups drained cottage cheese
4 cups hot mashed potatoes
½ cup sour cream
1 teaspoon salt
½ teaspoon white pepper
2 9-inch pastry-lined pie plates
3 tablespoons melted butter

Preheat oven to 350°.

Force the cottage cheese through a sieve; mix with the potatoes, sour cream, salt, and pepper until smooth. Fill the lined pie plates with the mixture and brush tops with the melted butter. Bake 35 minutes and remove 1 pie. Cool, wrap, seal, label, and freeze.

FOR TONIGHT'S DINNER

Continue baking the remaining pie 10 minutes longer. Serve warm.

TO SERVE FROM FROZEN STATE

Unwrap frozen pie; bake in a 350° oven 30 minutes, or until browned and hot.

Serves 6–8 each time.

BOSTON BAKED BEANS

5 cups white pea beans
2 teaspoons salt
1 cup chopped onions
1 pound thinly sliced salt pork
1 cup molasses
1 cup chili sauce
1 tablespoon dry mustard
1 teaspoon freshly ground black pepper

Wash the beans thoroughly, discarding any imperfect ones. Cover with water, bring to a boil, and let soak 1 hour. Drain. (If quick-cooking beans are used, omit this step.) Cover with fresh water and add the salt. Bring to a boil and cook over low heat 1 hour, or until tender but very firm. Drain.

The beans may be baked in 3 casseroles in which you will freeze them, or in one large bean pot, to be divided later for freezing. In either case, spread the onions on the bottom and arrange layers of beans and salt pork over them. Mix together the molasses, chili sauce, mustard, and pepper; pour over the beans. Add boiling water to cover. Cover and bake in a 250° oven for 3 hours, adding boiling water to keep the liquid level with the top. Remove 2 casseroles or two thirds of the bean mixture. Place over cold water or ice to cool quickly. Seal the casseroles, or pack beans into containers and seal. Freeze.

FOR TONIGHT'S DINNER
Continue baking the remaining beans, covered, for 30 minutes. Remove cover and bake 45 minutes longer.

TO SERVE FROM FROZEN STATE
Place one covered casserole (or turn beans into one) in a 250° oven for 1 hour. Remove cover and bake 30 minutes.
Serves 4–6 each time.

NOODLE-CHEESE CASSEROLE

2 pounds medium-fine noodles
½ pound cream cheese
2 cups drained cottage cheese
1½ cups sour cream
2 eggs
1½ teaspoons salt
¼ cup grated Parmesan cheese
2 tablespoons butter

Cook the noodles in salted water 2 minutes less than package suggests. Drain well.

Beat together the cream cheese, cottage cheese, sour cream, eggs, and salt. Mix with the noodles. Turn into 2 2-quart buttered casseroles. Sprinkle with the Parmesan cheese and dot with the butter. Bake both casseroles in a 350° oven 25 minutes. Remove 1; cool, wrap, seal, label, and freeze.

FOR TONIGHT'S DINNER

Bake the remaining casserole 15 minutes longer. Serve hot or warm.

TO SERVE FROM FROZEN STATE

Unwrap casserole and bake in a 325° oven 15 minutes. Sprinkle with ¼ cup grated Parmesan cheese and dot with 2 tablespoons butter. Raise heat to 350° and bake 25 minutes longer, or until browned and hot.

Serves 6–8 each time.

RISOTTO

¼ pound butter
1½ cups chopped onions
3 cups raw converted rice
8 cups hot fresh or canned beef broth
½ cup dry sherry
2 teaspoons salt
Grated Parmesan cheese

Melt the butter in a saucepan; sauté the onions until yellow and transparent. Stir in the rice until yellow. Add the broth, sherry, and salt. Cover, bring to a boil, and cook over low heat 15 minutes. Transfer half the rice to a bowl or saucepan and place in cold water or over ice to cool quickly. Pack into a container; seal, label, and freeze.

FOR TONIGHT'S DINNER

Continue cooking the remaining rice, covered, for 7 minutes, or until dry and tender but firm. Serve with Parmesan cheese, if desired.

TO SERVE FROM FROZEN STATE

Turn into a saucepan, cover, and cook over low heat 30 minutes, or until hot and tender but firm. Taste for seasoning, and serve with Parmesan cheese, if desired.

Serves 4–6 each time.

WHOLE-CRANBERRY SAUCE

1½ pounds cranberries
3 cups sugar
3 cups water

Pick over the cranberries, wash, and drain. Boil the sugar and water together for 5 minutes; add the cranberries and cook over high heat until skins burst open. Place pan in cold water or over ice to cool quickly. Pack into containers; seal, label, and freeze.

TO SERVE FROM FROZEN STATE
Remove from freezer 4 hours before serving. Keep covered until thawed.
Makes about 1½ quarts.

CRANBERRY-ORANGE RELISH

3 oranges
1½ pounds cranberries
3 cups sugar
¼ cup water

Cut the unpeeled oranges in pieces and remove seeds and membranes. Grind the oranges and cranberries in a food chopper. Boil the sugar and water together for 5 minutes and immediately pour over the fruit. Cool, pack into containers; seal, label, and freeze.

TO SERVE FROM FROZEN STATE
Remove from freezer 4 hours before serving. Keep covered until thawed.
Makes about 1½ quarts.

BREADS AND PANCAKES

Breads and rolls seem to improve with freezing, so always have a supply of home-baked or superior bakery products in the freezer. A delicious, crisp bread can be a delightful accent to an everyday or party meal.

Baked yeast breads and rolls should be cooled thoroughly before wrapping; then seal, label, and freeze. They thaw in 15 to 30 minutes, but may also be heated from the frozen state. Place in a 350° oven for 10 minutes, or until hot. Store up to 3 months.

Unbaked yeast breads and rolls may be baked from the frozen state, but do not store for more than 2 weeks, as the yeast action dies after that time.

Baked baking-powder breads thaw in 15 to 30 minutes, or may be heated in 10 minutes. Store up to 2 months. Do not freeze unbaked baking-powder breads.

Frozen pancakes are a great timesaver when the preparation is difficult. Follow instructions in individual recipes.

BAKING-POWDER BISCUITS

3 cups sifted flour
1 teaspoon salt
4 teaspoons baking powder
¼ pound butter
1⅓ cups light cream

Preheat oven to 425°.

Sift the flour, salt, and baking powder into a bowl; cut in the butter with a pastry blender or 2 knives until mixture is like coarse corn meal. Stir in the cream only until particles adhere. Turn out onto a lightly floured board and knead lightly. Roll out the dough ½ inch thick and cut with a 2-inch floured biscuit cutter. Transfer to an ungreased baking sheet. Brush with a little light cream. Bake 10 minutes and remove the number you want to freeze. Cool, wrap, seal, label, and freeze.

FOR IMMEDIATE SERVICE

Continue baking the remaining biscuits 3 minutes, or until browned. Serve hot.

TO SERVE FROM FROZEN STATE

Preheat oven to 425°.

Unwrap frozen biscuits and place on a baking sheet. Bake 5 minutes, or until browned and hot.

Makes about 30 biscuits.

DINNER ROLLS

¾ cup milk
4 tablespoons butter
4 tablespoons sugar
1½ teaspoons salt
2 cakes or packages yeast
¾ cup lukewarm water
4½ cups sifted flour
1 egg yolk
2 tablespoons light cream
Poppy seeds (optional)

Scald the milk and stir in the butter, sugar, and salt. Cool to lukewarm. In a mixing bowl, mix the yeast and water; let stand 5 minutes. Stir in the milk mixture and then half the flour. Beat with a wooden spoon until smooth, then work in the remaining flour. Turn out onto a floured surface and knead until smooth, about 10 minutes. Place in a buttered bowl, brush the top with melted butter, cover with a cloth, and let rise until double in bulk, about 1 hour.

Punch down; break off pieces and form them into rolls of any shape. Arrange on a buttered baking sheet, cover, and let rise in a warm place until double in bulk, about 45 minutes. Brush the tops with the egg yolk mixed with the cream, and sprinkle with the poppy seeds. Bake in a preheated 425° oven 12 minutes. Remove the ones you want to freeze, cool thoroughly on a cake rack; wrap, seal, label, and freeze.

FOR IMMEDIATE SERVICE
Continue baking the remaining rolls 5 minutes, or until browned.

TO SERVE FROM FROZEN STATE
Arrange unwrapped frozen rolls on a baking sheet. Bake in a preheated 400° oven 12 minutes, or until browned.
Makes 24–30.

RICH BISCUITS

4 cups sifted flour
1½ teaspoons salt
5 teaspoons baking powder
¾ cup (⅜ pound) butter
1½ cups heavy cream

Preheat oven to 450°.

Sift the flour, salt, and baking powder into a bowl; cut in the butter with a pastry blender or 2 knives. Make a well in the center and pour in 1¼ cups of the cream. Mix in the flour gently. Add enough of the remaining cream to make a soft but not sticky dough. Knead gently on a lightly floured surface. Roll out ½ inch thick and cut with a 2-inch floured cooky cutter. Arrange on a baking sheet, nearly touching for soft-sided biscuits, or 1 inch apart for crusty sides. Bake 12 minutes and remove number to be frozen. Cool thoroughly; wrap, seal, label, and freeze.

FOR IMMEDIATE SERVICE

Continue baking remaining biscuits 3 minutes longer, or until browned. Serve hot.

TO SERVE FROM FROZEN STATE

Preheat oven to 375°.

Arrange frozen biscuits on a baking sheet. Bake 8 minutes, or until browned and hot.

Makes about 36.

FRENCH BREAD

1 cake or envelope yeast
1½ cups lukewarm water
½ cup milk, scalded and cooled to lukewarm
2 tablespoons melted butter
1 tablespoon sugar
1½ teaspoons salt
5 cups sifted flour

Sprinkle the yeast into the water, let stand 5 minutes, and mix until smooth. In a bowl, combine the yeast mixture, milk, butter, sugar, and salt. Mix in the flour (it may not be necessary to use it all) until a sticky dough is formed. Turn out onto a floured surface and knead until smooth and elastic (about 10 minutes). Place the dough in a buttered bowl, cover with a cloth, and let rise in a warm place until double in bulk, about 2 hours. Punch down, cover, and let rise again for 1 hour.

Turn out onto a floured surface and knead again for a minute or two. Divide the dough in half and shape each half into a long, cylindrical loaf. Place on a buttered baking sheet. Cover and let rise again until double in bulk, about 1 hour. For an interesting design on top, cut small diagonal slits ¼ inch deep every few inches after half the rising time. Brush the top with milk. Bake in a preheated 400° oven 35 minutes. Remove one loaf to cool on a cake rack. When thoroughly cold, wrap, seal, label, and freeze.

FOR IMMEDIATE SERVICE
Continue baking the remaining loaf 15 minutes, or until golden brown. Cool on a cake rack.

TO SERVE FROM FROZEN STATE
Preheat oven to 400°.
Place unwrapped frozen loaf on baking sheet. Bake 20 minutes, or until golden brown.
Makes 2 10–12-inch loaves.
Note: Smaller loaves can be made, if more convenient for your family.

CHEESE BREAD

1 cup milk
1 tablespoon butter
2 teaspoons salt
1 cake or package yeast
2 tablespoons sugar
1¼ cups lukewarm water
6 cups sifted flour
2 cups (½ pound) grated natural Cheddar cheese
Salad oil

Scald the milk and stir in the butter and salt. Pour into a bowl and cool to lukewarm. Sprinkle the yeast and sugar into the water; stir until dissolved.

Beat 2 cups flour into the milk mixture until smooth; add the cheese and the yeast mixture; mix well. Add the remaining flour all at once, beating until smooth. If necessary, add a little more flour to make a fairly stiff dough.

Knead dough on a lightly floured surface until smooth and elastic. Place in a greased bowl, brush with salad oil, and cover with a cloth. Let rise in a warm place until double in bulk. Punch down and fold edges under. Cut in half and let stand 10 minutes. Shape into 2 loaves and place in 2 greased 9-inch loaf pans. Cover with the cloth and let rise in a warm place for 1 hour. Preheat oven to 400°. Bake 40 minutes, or until browned and sides are shrunk away from side of the pan. Cool on a cake rack.

The loaves may be sliced before freezing for easier service, or frozen in halves or whole. Wrap, seal, label, and freeze.

TO SERVE FROM FROZEN STATE

Remove slices 15 minutes before serving (or toast frozen), halves 45 minutes, and whole bread 1½ hours.

BLUEBERRY-NUT BREAD

4 cups sifted flour
1 teaspoon salt
1⅓ cups sugar
3 teaspoons baking powder
1 teaspoon baking soda
2 eggs, beaten
¼ cup melted butter
1½ cups orange juice
2 tablespoons grated orange rind
2 cups washed and dried blueberries
2 cups chopped walnuts or pecans

Preheat oven to 350°.
Sift together 3½ cups flour, the salt, sugar, baking powder, and soda. Mix in the eggs, then the butter, orange juice, and rind. Toss together the blueberries, nuts, and remaining flour; blend into the previous mixture. Divide evenly between 2 buttered 12-inch loaf pans. Bake 1 hour, or until a cake tester comes out clean. Cool on a cake rack for 10 minutes, then carefully turn out onto the rack. Cool thoroughly. Wrap, seal, label, and freeze.

TO SERVE FROM FROZEN STATE
Remove from freezer 2 hours before serving and place wrapped loaf on a cake rack.

BANANA BREAD

    3 cups sifted flour
    ¾ teaspoon salt
    ½ teaspoon baking soda
    4 teaspoons baking powder
    ⅔ cup butter
    1¼ cups sugar
    4 eggs
    2 cups mashed bananas

Preheat the oven to 350°.

Sift together the flour, salt, baking soda, and baking powder. Cream the butter, gradually adding the sugar and then the eggs; beat until light and fluffy. Beat in the flour mixture alternately with the bananas until smooth. Pour into 2 9-inch buttered loaf pans. Bake 1 hour, or until a cake tester comes out clean. Cool in the pans on a cake rack for 15 minutes, then carefully turn out. Cool for 4 hours before freezing. Wrap, seal, label, and freeze.

TO SERVE FROM FROZEN STATE

Remove loaf from freezer 1½ hours before you want to serve it. Makes 2 9-inch loaves.

BRIOCHE

1 cake or package yeast
2 tablespoons sugar
½ cup lukewarm water
5 cups sifted flour
½ teaspoon salt
¾ pound butter at room temperature
8 eggs
⅓ cup milk, scalded and cooled to lukewarm
1 egg yolk

Sprinkle the yeast and sugar into the water. Mix until smooth. Add 1 cup of the flour, mixing until a soft ball of dough is formed. Place in a buttered bowl, cover, and let rise in a warm place 1 hour.

Sift half the remaining flour and the salt into a bowl. Work in half the butter and 3 eggs; then mix in the milk. Work in the remaining butter, 3 eggs, and the remaining flour, mixing until smooth. Turn out onto a floured surface and knead and pick up and throw down until smooth, about 5 minutes. The dough will be sticky until kneaded enough. Work in the yeast mixture and remaining eggs and knead lightly for 2–3 minutes. Again the dough will be sticky until kneaded enough. Place in a buttered bowl, cover with a cloth, and let rise in a warm place for 3 hours. Punch down, cover again, and refrigerate overnight.

For small brioche, use individual brioche molds or fluted cup-cake tins. Break off pieces of dough, form into balls to half fill the molds. Make a crisscross cut on the top and press marble-sized balls into them. For large brioche, use larger molds, and half fill with large balls of dough. Make larger tops. Cover and let rise in a warm place until double in bulk, about 1 hour. Brush with the egg yolk.

Preheat oven to 425°.

Bake small ones 20 minutes (12 minutes for ones to be frozen) or until browned; large ones 50 minutes (40 minutes for those to be frozen) or until browned. Remove from mold. Cool the ones you want to freeze thoroughly on a cake rack. Wrap, seal, label, and freeze.

FOR IMMEDIATE SERVICE
Serve warm.

TO SERVE FROM FROZEN STATE
Place on a baking sheet and bake in a 400° oven 15 minutes, or until warm.

Makes about 24 small brioche or 3 large ones.

CROISSANTS

    2 cakes or packages yeast
    1 tablespoon sugar
    ¼ cup lukewarm water
    4 cups sifted flour
    ½ teaspoon salt
    1⅓ cups milk, scalded and cooled to lukewarm
    ¾ pound butter
    1 egg yolk
    1 tablespoon light cream

Sprinkle the yeast and sugar into the water in a bowl. Mix until smooth. Stir in 1 cup of the flour until a ball of dough is formed. Cut a cross in the top, cover with a towel, and let rise in a warm place until double in bulk, about 30 minutes.

Sift the remaining flour and salt into a bowl; gradually add the milk, mixing until a dough is formed. Beat in the yeast mixture and turn out onto a floured surface; knead lightly until smooth. Cover with a cloth and let stand 15 minutes.

Shape the butter into a flat square. Roll out the dough into a rectangle ½ inch thick; place the butter in the center. Fold over the 2 ends of the dough to make 3 layers. Turn open ends toward you. Roll out into a rectangle and fold into thirds again. Repeat this process 3 times. Wrap in a moist towel and chill for 4 hours or overnight. Roll out as above 3 times and chill 1 hour.

Roll out the dough ⅛ inch thick and cut into 6-inch squares, then cut diagonally to make triangles. Roll up from the long end and turn ends in to form crescents. Arrange on a lightly floured baking sheet. Cover and let rise in a warm place until double in bulk, about 1 hour. Brush with the egg yolk mixed with the cream.

Preheat oven to 400°.

Bake 5 minutes, then reduce heat to 350° and bake 10 minutes longer (5 minutes for those to be frozen) or until browned.

Transfer the croissants to a cake rack and thoroughly cool the ones to be frozen. Wrap, seal, label, and freeze.

FOR IMMEDIATE SERVICE

Serve warm.

TO SERVE FROM FROZEN STATE

Remove from freezer ½ hour before serving and bake, unwrapped, in a 400° oven 5 minutes.

Makes about 24.

PIZZA

1 cake or package yeast
½ teaspoon sugar
¾ cup lukewarm water
4 cups flour
1 teaspoon salt
6 tablespoons olive oil
3 cups tomato sauce
Oregano
Basil
Dried ground red peppers
2 cups diced mozzarella cheese

Soften the yeast and sugar in the water for 5 minutes. Sift the flour and salt onto a board and make a well in the center. Pour the yeast mixture into it. Work in the flour, kneading until smooth. Add 2 tablespoons olive oil and knead again for 10 minutes. Shape into a ball; cover with a towel and let rise in a warm place for 1 hour. Punch down the dough and roll out ¼ inch thick. The pizza can be baked any size, but for freezing, small ones are best.

Cut the dough with a 3-inch cooky cutter. Spread with the tomato sauce and sprinkle with the oregano, basil, red peppers, cheese, and finally the remaining olive oil. For immediate service, you can use anchovies, sliced Italian sausages or salami, chicken livers, etc., as well. Arrange all the pizzas on a baking sheet; place in an oven preheated to 450°. Bake the ones to be frozen 10 minutes and remove. Cool, pack into containers with double layers of freezer paper between, seal, label, and freeze.

FOR IMMEDIATE SERVICE
Preheat oven to 450°.
Bake a total of 18 minutes, or until browned. Serve hot.

TO SERVE FROM FROZEN STATE

Preheat oven to 450°.

Arrange anchovies, sliced Italian sausage, salami, or chicken livers on the frozen pizzas, if you like. Placc on a baking sheet and bake 10 minutes. Serve hot.

Makes about 48.

BLINTZES

Batter
2 cups flour
2 teaspoons salt
4 eggs
3 cups milk
2 tablespoons salad oil

Filling
1 cup drained cottage cheese
½ pound cream cheese
2 egg yolks
3 tablespoons sugar ⎫
1 teaspoon vanilla extract ⎭ optional

Sift the flour and 1 teaspoon salt into a bowl; beat in the eggs, milk, and oil. Chill 1 hour. The mixture should be the consistency of heavy cream, so add a little more milk if necessary.

Melt a little butter in a 7-inch skillet, and pour in about 1 tablespoon of the batter. Tip pan quickly to coat the bottom. When the pancake is browned on the bottom, turn it out onto a plate or napkin, browned side down. Prepare the balance, adding more butter as necessary, and stacking the pancakes. Reserve 1 tablespoon batter.

Beat together the cottage cheese, cream cheese, egg yolks, remaining salt, and the sugar and vanilla if you like blintzes sweet. Place a tablespoon of the mixture on each pancake, turn opposite ends in, and roll up. Seal with a little of the batter. Chill the number you want to freeze; pack in a container with double layers of foil or freezer paper between, wrap, and freeze.

FOR TONIGHT'S DINNER

Melt some butter in a skillet; brown the blintzes in it on both sides. Serve hot or cold with sour cream.

TO SERVE FROM FROZEN STATE

Heat ¼ cup salad oil or shortening in a skillet; add 3 table-spoons butter. Carefully place the blintzes in it. Bake over low heat until browned on both sides and hot.

Makes about 24.

DATE-NUT LOAF

3 cups sifted flour
3 teaspoons baking soda
½ teaspoon salt
2 cups pitted dates
2 cups coarsely chopped walnuts
1½ cups boiling water
½ cup (¼ pound) butter
4 eggs
1½ cups brown sugar, firmly packed
2 teaspoons vanilla extract

Preheat oven to 350°.

Sift together the flour, baking soda, and salt. Cut up the dates and combine with the walnuts, boiling water, and butter. Let stand 15 minutes.

Beat the eggs and gradually add the brown sugar and vanilla. Mix in the flour mixture until smooth. Stir in the date mixture until just blended. Turn into 2 9-inch buttered loaf pans. Bake 1 hour, or until a cake tester comes out clean. Cool in the pans on a rack for 15 minutes, then remove from pans. Let cool 4 hours before freezing. The loaf may be sliced before freezing or frozen whole. Wrap, seal, label, and freeze.

TO SERVE FROM FROZEN STATE

Remove from freezer 1½ hours before you want to serve it. Or unwrap and place in a 350° oven for 15 minutes.

Makes 2 9-inch loaves.

SAUCES

A delicious sauce can turn plain meat or chicken into an epi-
curean dish, and most sauces require long cooking. So prepare
them in large quantities and freeze for future use. Always skim the
fat before freezing. Pack into jars or freezer containers, allowing
1 inch headroom. When ready to reheat, hold the container under
hot running water to loosen, then turn into a saucepan. Cook
over very low heat until hot, stirring frequently.

BROWN STOCK

    3 pounds beef bones
    2 pounds veal bones
    3 onions, sliced
    1 carrot, sliced
    5 quarts water
    2 teaspoons salt
    3 stalks celery
    4 sprigs parsley
    1 bay leaf

Put the bones, onions, and carrot on a flat pan; bake in a 400°
oven until dark brown on all sides. Transfer to a saucepan and
add the water, salt, celery, parsley, and bay leaf. Bring to a boil
and skim the top. Cook over low heat 4 hours. Strain and cool;
skim the fat. Pour into 6 pint containers; seal, label, and freeze
until needed for making soups or sauces.

Makes 6 pints.

BROWN SAUCE

¼ pound beef fat
1 cup chopped onions
½ cup grated carrots
½ cup flour
6 cups hot Brown Stock or canned beef broth
2 stalks celery
3 sprigs parsley
1 bay leaf
⅛ teaspoon thyme
3 tablespoons tomato paste

Melt the fat in a saucepan; sauté the onions and carrots 10 minutes. Blend in the flour until brown. Add the stock, stirring steadily to the boiling point. Add the celery, parsley, bay leaf, and thyme. Cook over low heat 2 hours. Stir in the tomato paste and cook 1 hour longer. Strain, cool, and skim the fat. Pour into 2 pint containers; seal, label, and freeze until needed to heat and serve or use in other sauces, like the following:

MUSHROOM SAUCE
4 tablespoons butter
¾ pound mushrooms, sliced
3 tablespoons minced shallots or onions
½ cup Madeira or dry sherry
1½ cups Brown Sauce

Melt the butter in a saucepan; sauté the mushrooms and shallots 5 minutes. Mix in the wine and Brown Sauce; bring to a boil and cook over low heat 5 minutes. Taste for seasoning.

Makes about 2 cups. Delicious with meat and poultry dishes, particularly steak or roast fillet.

COURT BOUILLON

3 pounds fish heads, bones, and trimmings
1 tablespoon butter
½ cup minced onions
1 carrot, sliced
4 sprigs parsley
1½ quarts dry white wine
1½ quarts water
1 teaspoon salt
¼ teaspoon white pepper

Buy the heads and trimmings of white-meat fish for more delicate flavor. Melt the butter in a saucepan; add the fish, onions, carrot, and parsley. Cover and cook over low heat 10 minutes. Add the wine, water, salt, and pepper; bring to a boil and cook over low heat 30 minutes. Strain. Cool; pour into 5 pint jars, allowing 1 inch headroom. Cover, seal, label, and freeze. Use as directed in recipes.

SPAGHETTI SAUCE

½ cup olive oil or salad oil
3 cups diced onions
1 pound ground beef
2 carrots, grated
½ cup chopped parsley
3 29-ounce cans Italian-style tomatoes
½ cup dry white wine
1 tablespoon salt
1 teaspoon freshly ground black pepper
1 teaspoon oregano
1 pound mushrooms, chopped
2 cloves garlic, minced

Heat the oil in a saucepan; sauté the onions 10 minutes. Add the beef and cook over high heat, stirring constantly until meat loses its redness. Add the carrots, parsley, tomatoes, wine, salt, and pepper. Cover and cook over low heat 2 hours. Add the oregano and mushrooms. Cook 30 minutes.

Remove half the sauce. Chill and pack in a jar or freezer container, allowing 1 inch headroom. Seal, label, and freeze.

FOR IMMEDIATE SERVICE
Add the garlic to the remaining sauce and cook 1 hour longer.

TO SERVE FROM FROZEN STATE
Turn into a saucepan. Add 2 minced cloves garlic. Cover and cook over low heat 1 hour.

Makes about 2 quarts.

HOLLANDAISE SAUCE

8 egg yolks
2 tablespoons lemon juice
1 teaspoon salt
½ pound sweet butter
4 tablespoons heavy cream

Beat the egg yolks, lemon juice, and salt in the top of a double boiler. Divide the butter in thirds and add 1 part to the egg yolks. Place over hot, not boiling, water and stir constantly with a wooden spoon until butter is absorbed. Add another third of the butter and stir constantly again until absorbed. Add the remaining butter, stirring again until absorbed. (Add a little cold water to the underpart of the double boiler if it reaches the boiling point, but make sure water is never high enough to touch top part of double boiler.) Mix until thickened and smooth, then stir in the cream. Remove half the sauce and cool. Pack in a container; seal, label, and freeze.

FOR IMMEDIATE SERVICE
Serve as soon as possible.

TO SERVE FROM FROZEN STATE
Turn into the top of the double boiler. Place over hot water and cook, stirring frequently, until thawed.
Makes about 2 cups sauce.

DESSERTS

Every dinner can end with a wonderful dessert, right out of your freezer. A rainy day is the perfect time to stock a dwindling supply. And of course take advantage of the season to freeze fruit pies and compotes.

CAKES

Baked cakes must be cooled thoroughly before wrapping. Because cakes do not freeze solidly, it is advisable to protect them from damage by packing in a firm container, such as a cardboard box or aluminum-foil container. Cakes may be cut into individual servings and then frozen, if preferred. This method is desirable for small families. Wrap the cake carefully in moisture- vapor-proof material; seal, label, and freeze. Cakes defrost in about 45 minutes. Store up to 3 months. Fruitcakes keep for 1 year.

Frosted cakes may be frozen, but not if made with a 7-minute or egg-white frosting. Butter frostings, confectioners'-sugar and candy types freeze well. Place the cake in the freezer, unwrapped, until firm, about 2–3 hours. Then wrap as described above. Keeps up to 1 month.

COOKIES

Cookies may be frozen baked or unbaked. Cool baked cookies before wrapping. Pack in a solid container in layers, with freezer paper or aluminum foil between each layer. Wrap the container in moisture- vaporproof material, label, and freeze. Baked cookies defrost in about 15 minutes. Keep up to 9 months.

Unbaked cooky dough should be rolled and cut into shapes. Pack in layers, as described above, then freeze. When wanted, bake without defrosting. Store up to 6 months.

Bulk cooky dough may be frozen, but it is not as practical a method as the previous two. The dough must be defrosted before rolling and cutting, so use this method only if you have left-over dough and lack time to roll it before freezing. If desired, form the dough into long rolls or bricks; wrap and freeze. When ready to bake, slice while still frozen. Place on greased baking sheet and bake.

PIES

Pies may be frozen baked or unbaked. The pastry is usually flakier when frozen unbaked, but for emergency use, the baked method is quicker.

Unbaked fruit or mince pies may be prepared in the usual manner, but don't cut vents in the top before freezing. Wrap in moisture- vaporproof wrap, slip into a carton to prevent possible damage. Label and freeze. When ready to bake, make vents in the frozen pie and bake in a 425° oven for 50 minutes, or until browned. Keep up to 3 months.

Baked fruit or mince pies should be cooled before wrapping; follow above procedure. Defrost for 2 hours, or heat in a 375° oven for 30 minutes. Keep up to 3 months.

Chiffon pies must be cool and set before wrapping as above. Don't decorate with whipped cream or meringue before freezing. To defrost, unwrap and place in refrigerator for 1½ hours. Decorate as desired and serve. Keep up to 1 month.

Lemon meringue pies should be cool and set before wrapping. Do not cover with meringue before freezing. When ready to use, spread meringue on the frozen pie and bake in a 350° oven for 20 minutes. Let cool for 1 hour. Store up to 2 months.

Pumpkin pies must be cool and set before wrapping; follow procedure described above. When ready to serve, unwrap and let thaw for 1 hour, or heat in a 375° oven 20 minutes. Keep no longer than 2 months.

Pie shells may be frozen baked or unbaked. Freeze before wrapping. You can then remove them from the pie plates (if not aluminum foil or paper) and stack carefully with crumpled waxed paper or cardboard between each. Place in a box or cardboard container, or the pie shells may be damaged during storage. When ready to use, thaw baked shells at room temperature for 30 minutes. As mentioned above, unbaked frozen shells are flakier and more desirable; bake these in a 425° oven 20 minutes, pricking the shells after 5 minutes of baking time. Store no longer than 3 months.

ANGEL SPONGECAKE

1 cup sifted cake flour
¼ teaspoon salt
½ cup water
1¼ cups sugar
1 teaspoon cream of tartar
8 egg yolks
8 egg whites
1 teaspoon vanilla extract

Preheat the oven to 300°. Sift the flour and salt 3 times. Combine the water, sugar, and ½ teaspoon cream of tartar in a saucepan. Bring to a boil and cook over low heat until a thread is formed when a fork is lifted from the syrup.

Beat the egg yolks until thick, then gradually beat in the syrup. Continue beating until cool. Fold in the flour and salt. Beat the egg whites and remaining cream of tartar until stiff but not dry. Fold into the previous mixture with the vanilla. Divide mixture between 2 6-inch tube pans. Bake 1 hour, or until a cake tester comes out clean. Invert on a cake rack and let cool in the pans before removing. Wrap, seal, label, and freeze.

TO SERVE FROM FROZEN STATE
Remove from freezer 1½ hours before serving. Leave wrapped and place on a cake rack to thaw.

BUTTER SPONGECAKE

8 egg yolks
1 cup sugar
2 teaspoons vanilla extract
1¾ cups sifted cake flour
8 egg whites
½ cup melted cooled butter

Preheat the oven to 350°. Butter 3 9-inch layer-cake pans and dust lightly with flour.

Beat the egg yolks and sugar until fluffy and very pale in color. Mix in the vanilla. Fold in ⅓ of the flour at a time.

Beat the egg whites until stiff but not dry, and fold into the yolk mixture carefully but thoroughly. Then fold in the butter. Divide the mixture among the 3 pans. Bake 30 minutes, or until a cake tester comes out clean. Cool on a cake rack for 10 minutes, then turn out onto the rack and cool thoroughly. Wrap, seal, label, and freeze as is, or split and ice with Mocha Frosting:

½ pound sweet butter
½ cup sugar
1 tablespoon unsweetened cocoa
1 tablespoon instant coffee
1 tablespoon boiling water

Cream the butter, gradually adding the sugar and cocoa. Dissolve the coffee in the water and blend into the butter mixture. Ice the cake and freeze before wrapping.

TO SERVE FROM FROZEN STATE

Remove unfrosted cake 1 hour before serving and leave it wrapped. Place on a cake rack to thaw. Decorate as you like.

Remove frosted cake 2 hours before serving and unwrap immediately. Place on a cake rack.

CHOCOLATE ROLL

12 ounces sweet chocolate
⅓ cup brewed coffee
10 egg yolks
1½ cups sugar
10 egg whites
Unsweetened cocoa
3 cups heavy cream, whipped
2 teaspoons vanilla extract

Preheat the oven to 350°. Oil 2 jelly-roll pans (12 × 18 inches), line them with waxed paper, and butter the paper.

Melt the chocolate in the coffee over low heat; cool. Beat the egg yolks, gradually adding the sugar. Beat until thick and light. Mix in the chocolate. Beat the egg whites until stiff but not dry; fold into the chocolate mixture lightly but thoroughly. Turn into the prepared pans and spread evenly. Bake 15 minutes, or until a cake tester comes out clean. Do not overbake. Cover the cakes with damp towels and place in the refrigerator for 1 hour.

Sprinkle 2 pieces of waxed paper, a little longer than the cake, with cocoa. Carefully turn out the cakes and gently peel the paper from them. Mix the whipped cream and vanilla and spread over the cakes. Roll up the long way, by gently raising the edge of the waxed paper. Don't worry if the roll cracks—patch it with a little more cocoa. Place 1 roll on a foil-covered piece of cardboard. Wrap, seal, label, and freeze.

FOR IMMEDIATE SERVICE

Chill the remaining roll for 2 hours; slice and serve with chocolate sauce, if desired.

TO SERVE FROM FROZEN STATE

Remove roll from freezer 1 hour before serving. Slice and serve as above.

Serves 10–12 each time.

CARAMEL-NUT CAKE

3 cups sifted cake flour
3 teaspoons baking powder
½ pound (1 cup) butter
4 cups dark-brown sugar, firmly packed
8 egg yolks
½ cup milk
3 teaspoons vanilla extract
2 cups chopped walnuts
8 egg whites
¾ teaspoon salt

Preheat the oven to 375°. Butter 4 8-inch layer-cake pans and dust lightly with flour.

Sift the flour and baking powder together. Cream the butter, gradually adding the sugar. Beat until fluffy. Add 1 egg yolk at a time, beating well after each addition. Add the flour mixture alternately with the milk, beating until smooth. Stir in the vanilla and nuts.

Beat the egg whites and salt until stiff but not dry; fold into the butter mixture. Divide among the 4 pans. Bake 20 minutes, or until a cake tester comes out clean. Turn out onto a cake rack until cold. Make 2 cakes, filling and frosting the layers with the following:

4 cups dark brown sugar, firmly packed
2 cups light cream
6 tablespoons butter
2 teaspoons vanilla extract
¾ cup chopped walnuts

Combine the sugar and cream in a saucepan. Cook over low heat, stirring steadily, until sugar melts. Then cook until a little dropped in cold water forms a soft ball, or until candy ther-mometer reaches 230°. Remove from the heat and stir in the butter. Let cool, then beat in the vanilla until creamy. Stir in the nuts. If too thick for easy spreading, add a little more cream.

Freeze one cake; wrap, seal, label, and return to freezer.

FOR IMMEDIATE SERVICE

Place cake in refrigerator until icing is firm. Cut and serve.

TO SERVE FROM FROZEN STATE

Unwrap cake and place on a cake rack 2 hours before serving. Serves 6–8 each time.

NUT ROLL

12 egg yolks
1½ cups sugar
3 cups ground nuts
2 teaspoons baking powder
2 teaspoons vanilla extract
12 egg whites
Confectioners' sugar
3 cups heavy cream
3 tablespoons cognac

Preheat the oven to 350°. Butter 2 jelly-roll pans (11 × 18 inches); line them with waxed paper, and butter the paper.

Beat the egg yolks and sugar together until thick and light. Toss the nuts with the baking powder and stir into the yolk mixture with the vanilla. Beat the egg whites until stiff but not dry. Fold into the nut mixture. Spread evenly on the prepared pan. Bake 15 minutes, or until a cake tester comes out clean. Don't overbake.

Remove from the oven and cover with a damp towel until completely cool; loosen from the pans. Sprinkle confectioners' sugar heavily on two pieces of waxed paper. Turn out the cakes and carefully peel the waxed paper from them. Whip the cream with three tablespoons confectioners' sugar. Stir in the cognac; spread on the cakes and roll up lengthwise. The cake is very delicate, so don't worry if it cracks slightly in rolling. Wrap one cake in foil or freezer paper; seal, label, and freeze.

FOR IMMEDIATE SERVICE

Cover the roll with additional whipped cream or shaved chocolate, if desired. Chill for 1 hour before serving.

TO SERVE FROM FROZEN STATE

Remove from freezer 30 minutes before serving time and place on a cake rack. Serve as above.

Serves 8–10 each time.

FRUIT-NUT CAKE

2¼ cups sifted flour
½ teaspoon salt
1½ teaspoons baking powder
1¾ cups chopped mixed candied fruits
1 cup seedless white raisins
1 cup crushed walnuts
1 cup dried, flaked coconut
¼ pound butter
1 cup sugar
3 eggs
1 egg yolk
¼ cup orange juice
¼ cup cognac

Preheat the oven to 300°. Grease 3 9-inch loaf pans and line them with waxed paper; grease the paper.

Sift together the flour, salt, and baking powder into a bowl. Add the candied fruits, raisins, walnuts, and coconut. Toss together to coat the fruits and nuts with the flour mixture.

Cream the butter, gradually adding the sugar; beat until light. Beat in the eggs and egg yolk until light and fluffy. Mix in the orange juice and cognac. Combine the butter mixture with the fruit mixture, stirring until blended. Divide among the 3 pans. Bake 1½ hours, or until a cake tester comes out clean and cakes shrink from sides of pans. Cool on a cake rack and turn out. Be sure the cakes are cold before wrapping. Seal, label, and freeze.

FOR IMMEDIATE SERVICE
Let the cake ripen overnight before serving.

TO SERVE FROM FROZEN STATE
Remove from freezer 6 hours before serving. Place wrapped cake on a rack to thaw.

PASTRY FOR PIES OR TARTS

You may prepare the pastry as directed on shortening cans or make either of the following ones, which freeze perfectly and provide a delicate flaky result:

SOUR-CREAM PASTRY
   2 cups sifted flour
   ½ teaspoon salt
   ½ pound sweet butter
   6 tablespoons sour cream

Sift the flour and salt into a bowl; cut in the butter with a pastry blender or work it in by hand. Add the sour cream, mixing lightly until a ball of dough is formed. Wrap in waxed paper or foil and chill overnight or for at least 3 hours. Divide dough in half and roll out as thin as possible. Proceed as directed in recipes.
   Makes 2 9-inch shells or 1 9-inch covered pie.

TART PASTRY
   2 cups sifted flour
   ¼ teaspoon salt
   2 tablespoons sugar
   ½ pound sweet butter (softened to room temperature)
   2 egg yolks
   2 tablespoons ice water

Sift the flour, salt, and sugar into a bowl or onto a board. Make a well in the center and into it put the butter, egg yolks, and water. Work in the flour until a ball of dough is formed. Wrap in waxed paper or foil and chill overnight or for at least 3 hours. Roll out ⅛ inch thick on a lightly floured surface; fit into a buttered 9-inch pie plate. Flute the edges and chill 30 minutes. Wrap, seal, label, and freeze.

FOR IMMEDIATE SERVICE

If a prebaked shell is required, prick the bottom and place another pie plate over the shell, or cover with waxed paper and fill with beans or rice to keep shell in place and avoid shrinkage. Bake in a preheated 400° oven 20 minutes, or until browned. Carefully remove weight and cool on a cake rack.

TO BAKE FROM FROZEN STATE

Unwrap shell and weight it as above. Bake in a preheated 425° oven 20 minutes, or until browned.

Makes 2 9-inch pie shells.

APPLE PIE

Make as many pies as you like at one time when apples are at their best. Freeze until needed, then bake and have fresh apple pie.

Pastry for 2-crust 9-inch pie
1 tablespoon melted butter
2 pounds apples
½ teaspoon ascorbic acid (buy in drugstore), powdered or liquid
2 teaspoons lemon juice
¾ cup sugar
2 tablespoons flour
½ teaspoon cinnamon ⎫
¼ teaspoon nutmeg　⎬ optional
1 tablespoon butter　⎭

Roll out half the pastry to fit the pie plate; brush the bottom of the crust with the melted butter and chill for 30 minutes.

Pare the apples and slice thin. Toss lightly with the ascorbic acid dissolved in the lemon juice, the sugar, flour, cinnamon, and nutmeg.

Fill the pie plate with the mixture, dot with butter, and cover with the remaining thinly rolled out pastry. Seal the edges well; wrap, seal, label, and freeze.

FOR IMMEDIATE SERVICE

Cut a few slits in the top of the pastry. Brush with a little heavy cream. Bake in a 425° oven 45 minutes, or until browned and fruit is tender. Cool on a cake rack and serve warm or cold.

TO SERVE FROM FROZEN STATE

Unwrap pie and make a few slits in the top. Brush with a little heavy cream. Bake in a 425° oven 55 minutes, or until browned and fruit is tender.

PEACH PIE

¾ teaspoon ascorbic acid (buy in drugstore)
1 tablespoon water
Pastry for 2-crust pie
4 cups sliced peaches
⅔ cup sugar
3 tablespoons flour
⅛ teaspoon salt
¼ teaspoon nutmeg ⎫
¼ teaspoon cinnamon ⎬ optional

1 tablespoon butter

Dissolve the ascorbic acid in the water.

Roll out half the pastry to fit a 9-inch pie plate. Toss together the peaches, ascorbic acid, sugar, flour, salt, nutmeg and cinnamon. Fill the pie plate and dot with the butter. Roll out the remaining pastry and cover the fruit, sealing the edges well. Wrap, seal, label, and freeze.

FOR IMMEDIATE SERVICE

Preheat oven to 425°.

Slit the top of the pastry in several places and brush with a little heavy cream. Bake 45 minutes, or until browned. Cool on a cake rack; serve warm or cold.

TO SERVE FROM FROZEN STATE

Preheat oven to 425°.

Unwrap frozen pie; slit the top and brush with a little heavy cream. Bake 55 minutes or until browned.

BERRY PIE

Pastry for 2-crust pie
4 cups blueberries, raspberries, or blackberries
3 tablespoons flour
¾ cup sugar
⅛ teaspoon salt
1 teaspoon almond extract
2 teaspoons lemon juice
1 tablespoon butter

Roll out half the pastry to fit a 9-inch pie plate. Toss together the berries, flour, sugar, salt, almond extract, and lemon juice. Fill the pie shell and dot with the butter. Roll out the remaining pastry and cover the fruit, sealing the edges well. Wrap, seal, label, and freeze.

FOR IMMEDIATE SERVICE
Preheat oven to 425°.
Make a few slits in the top crust, brush with heavy cream, and bake 45 minutes, or until browned. Cool on a cake rack and serve warm or cold.

TO SERVE FROM FROZEN STATE
Preheat oven to 425°.
Unwrap frozen pie and slit the top; brush with a little heavy cream. Bake in oven 55 minutes, or until browned.

CHERRY TART

2 9-inch pastry-lined pie plates
2 tablespoons melted butter
3 pounds black cherries
1 cup sugar
2 tablespoons flour
2 teaspoons lemon juice
¼ teaspoon almond extract
½ cup currant jelly
2 tablespoons water

Brush the bottom of pastry with the butter and chill 30 minutes.

Pit the cherries and toss with the sugar, flour, lemon juice, and almond extract. Fill the pie plates. Wrap, seal, label, and freeze 1 or both.

FOR IMMEDIATE SERVICE

Preheat oven to 375°.

Bake the pie 30 minutes, or until pastry is browned and cherries tender. Cool on a cake rack.

Melt the jelly in the water, brush the cherries with it several times to glaze. Chill until set. Decorate with whipped cream, if desired.

TO SERVE FROM FROZEN STATE

Preheat oven to 400°.

Unwrap pie and bake 35 minutes, or until pastry is browned and cherries tender. Glaze as above.

PEACH TART

- 1½ teaspoons ascorbic acid (buy in drugstore)
- 1 tablespoon water
- 2 9-inch pastry-lined pie plates
- 2 tablespoons melted butter
- 6 cups sliced peaches
- 1 cup sugar
- 1 teaspoon cinnamon
- 1 egg yolk
- ¼ cup heavy cream

Dissolve the ascorbic acid in the water.

Brush the bottom of the pastry with the butter; chill 30 minutes.

Toss together the peaches, ascorbic acid, sugar, and cinnamon. Fill the pie plates. Wrap, seal, label, and freeze one or both.

FOR IMMEDIATE SERVICE

Preheat oven to 375°

Bake the pie 20 minutes. Beat the egg yolk and the cream together and pour over the fruit. Bake 15 minutes longer, or until pastry is browned and fruit tender. Serve warm or cold.

TO SERVE FROM FROZEN STATE

Preheat oven to 400°.

Unwrap frozen pie and bake 25 minutes. Pour over the fruit 1 egg yolk beaten with ¼ cup heavy cream and bake 15 minutes longer, or until pastry is browned and fruit tender.

LEMON MERINGUE PIE

2 baked 9-inch pie shells
6 eggs
½ cup sifted cornstarch
2⅓ cups sugar
½ teaspoon salt
2½ cups water
½ cup lemon juice
2 tablespoons butter or margarine
2 tablespoons grated lemon rind

Separate the eggs and place 3 of the whites in a freezer container. Freeze. Beat the yolks slightly.

Combine the cornstarch, 2 cups sugar, and ¼ teaspoon salt in the top of a double boiler. Gradually add the water, lemon juice, and butter. Place over hot water and cook, stirring constantly, until thick. Stir in the rind and cool. Fill the pie shells evenly. Freeze 1 pie, then wrap in moisture- vaporproof wrap and return to freezer.

FOR TONIGHT'S DINNER

Preheat oven to 350°.

Beat the remaining 3 egg whites and remaining salt until frothy. Gradually add the remaining 6 tablespoons sugar, beating well after each addition. Continue beating until stiff but not dry. Cover the remaining pie with it and bake about 10 minutes, or until delicately browned. Cool.

TO SERVE FROM FROZEN STATE

Remove the egg whites from freezer and let thaw about 3 hours. Follow instructions for making the meringue and cover frozen pie with it. Bake in a 350° oven 20 minutes. Cool and serve.

Serves 6–8 each time.

PUMPKIN PIE

- 2 9-inch pastry-lined pie plates
- 2 tablespoons melted butter
- 5 eggs
- 2 cups brown sugar, firmly packed
- 1 teaspoon salt
- 1½ teaspoons cinnamon
- ¾ teaspoon powdered ginger
- ½ teaspoon nutmeg
- 3½ cups cooked or canned puréed pumpkin
- 3 cups heavy cream
- ¼ cup cognac

Brush the bottom of the pastry with the butter. Chill 30 minutes.
Beat the eggs, brown sugar, salt, cinnamon, ginger, and nutmeg until light and fluffy. Mix in the pumpkin, cream, and cognac. Pour into the lined pie plates. Bake in a preheated 425° oven 15 minutes. Reduce heat to 350° and bake 30 minutes longer, or until a knife inserted in the center comes out clean. Cool on a cake rack. Be sure the pie to be frozen is cold before wrapping. Seal, label, and freeze.

FOR IMMEDIATE SERVICE
Serve pie warm, with whipped cream, if desired.

TO SERVE FROM FROZEN STATE
Unwrap pie and thaw 2 hours before serving. Or to serve warm, place in a 350° oven for 20 minutes.

CHEESE PIE

2 pounds cream cheese
1½ cups sugar
4 eggs
¼ cup heavy cream
4 teaspoons vanilla extract
2 9-inch pastry-lined pie plates
1 cup sour cream

Preheat oven to 350°.

Beat the cheese and the sugar (reserving 2 tablespoons) until smooth. Add the eggs, cream, and 2 teaspoons vanilla, beating until light and fluffy. Pour into the pie plates. Bake 20 minutes. While the pie is baking, mix the sour cream with the remaining sugar and vanilla. At the end of the 20 minutes, raise the heat to 425°. Spread the sour-cream mixture over the tops of the pies and bake 5 minutes. Cool. Wrap 1 pie; seal, label, and freeze.

FOR IMMEDIATE SERVICE

Chill the pie 2 hours before serving.

TO SERVE FROM FROZEN STATE

Remove pie from freezer 3 hours before serving time. Let thaw on a cake rack.

Serves 6–8 each time.

PECAN PIE

- 2½ cups sifted flour
- ½ teaspoon salt
- ⅔ cup shortening
- ⅓ cup ice water
- ½ cup butter
- 1⅓ cups brown sugar, firmly packed
- 1½ cups dark corn syrup
- 6 eggs
- 2 teaspoons vanilla extract
- 2 cups shelled pecans

Sift the flour and salt into a bowl; cut in the shortening with a pastry blender or 2 knives. Add the water, tossing lightly until a ball of dough is formed. Wrap in waxed paper and chill 1 hour. Divide the dough in half and roll out to fit two 8-inch pie plates (one aluminum foil, if possible). Preheat oven to 400°.

Cream the butter, gradually adding the sugar. Beat until light and fluffy. Add the corn syrup, eggs, and vanilla. Beat again. Stir in the nuts. Pour equal amounts into the lined pie plates. Bake in a 400° oven 10 minutes. Reduce the heat to 350° and bake 25 minutes. Remove one pie and cool on a cake rack. Wrap in moisture- vaporproof wrap, label, and freeze.

FOR TONIGHT'S DINNER

Bake the remaining pie 5 minutes longer, or until a knife comes out clean. Cool.

TO SERVE FROM FROZEN STATE

Preheat oven to 350°.

Unwrap frozen pie and bake 20 minutes. Serve with whipped cream if desired.

Serves 6–8 each time.

HONEY SQUARES

4 cups sifted cake flour
¼ teaspoon salt
1 teaspoon nutmeg
1 teaspoon cinnamon
1 teaspoon cream of tartar
1 teaspoon baking soda
½ pound (1 cup) butter
½ cup dark brown sugar, firmly packed
4 eggs
¾ cup honey
1 cup sour cream
16 blanched almonds, split

Preheat the oven to 350°. Butter 2 8-inch square pans and dust lightly with flour.

Sift together the flour, salt, nutmeg, cinnamon, cream of tartar, and baking soda.

Melt the butter and dissolve the sugar in it; cool. Beat the eggs, gradually adding the honey; beat until light and fluffy. Beat in the sour cream and then the butter mixture. Stir in the flour mixture gradually. Divide between the 2 pans. Arrange the halved almonds in regular design. Bake 40 minutes, or until a cake tester comes out clean. Cool on a cake rack for 10 minutes, then carefully turn out onto the rack. Cool thoroughly. Cut each cake into 16 squares. Wrap the number you want to freeze; seal, label, and freeze.

FOR IMMEDIATE SERVICE

Store the remaining squares in an airtight container for 24 hours before serving.

TO SERVE FROM FROZEN STATE

Remove squares from freezer 2 hours before serving.
Makes 32 2-inch squares.

DANISH PASTRY

4½ cups sifted flour
¾ pound (1½ cups) butter
2 cakes or packages yeast
¼ cup lukewarm water
5 tablespoons sugar
½ teaspoon salt
1 cup milk, scalded and cooled
1 egg, beaten

Sift ⅓ cup flour into a bowl. Cut in the butter with a pastry blender or 2 knives. Place between 2 sheets of waxed paper and roll into a 10 × 6-inch rectangle. Chill.

Combine the yeast, water, and 1 tablespoon sugar; let stand 5 minutes, then mix until smooth. Pour into a bowl and mix in the remaining sugar, the salt, milk, and egg. Add the remaining flour gradually, beating with a wooden spoon until a soft dough is formed. It may not be necessary to add all the flour. Knead the dough on a floured surface until smooth.

Roll out the dough into a 12-inch square. Place the butter mixture on one half and fold the other half over it. Press the edges together to seal. Roll out the dough as thin as possible and fold into thirds. Turn the open ends toward you and roll out again. Repeat 3 times. Chill 1 hour or longer.

Divide the dough in thirds and roll out ⅛ inch thick. Cut into desired shapes, fill with selected filling, and shape. Pack the number you want to freeze in containers with double layers of foil or freezer paper between the layers. Wrap, seal, label, and freeze.

FOR IMMEDIATE SERVICE

Arrange remaining pastries on a baking sheet. Cover with a cloth and let rise for 30 minutes. Preheat oven to 400°.

Brush the tops with 1 beaten egg mixed with a little milk. Bake 5 minutes, reduce heat to 350° and bake 15 minutes, or until browned. Mix 1 cup confectioners' sugar with 2 tablespoons cream and brush the tops while hot.

TO SERVE FROM FROZEN STATE

Preheat oven to 400°.

Arrange frozen pastries on a baking sheet. Brush with 1 beaten egg mixed with 1 tablespoon milk. Bake 5 minutes; reduce heat to 350° and bake 15 minutes longer, or until browned. Glaze as above, if desired.

Makes about 24 pastries.

Note: Frozen unbaked pastries should not be stored for more than 2 weeks.

DANISH PASTRY FILLING

NUT FILLING
  2 cups walnuts, pecans, or blanched almonds
  1 cup sugar
  2 eggs

Grind the nuts in an electric blender, Mouli grater, or food chopper. Mix in the sugar and eggs until smooth.

CHEESE FILLING
  2 cups cottage cheese
  2 eggs
  3 tablespoons sugar
  ⅛ teaspoon salt
  1 teaspoon vanilla extract

Mix all the ingredients together.

PRUNE FILLING
  2 4-ounce jars (baby food) puréed prunes
  ½ cup ground nuts
  2 teaspoons grated orange rind

Cook the prunes until thickened. Stir in the nuts and orange rind.

POPPY-SEED FILLING
  2 cups ground poppy seeds
  ¾ cup honey
  ¼ cup milk
  3 tablespoons sugar
  1 egg

Cook the poppy seeds, honey, milk, and sugar until thick. Cool slightly and beat in the egg.

CREAM PUFFS OR ÉCLAIRS

½ pound butter
2 cups water
1 teaspoon salt
1 teaspoon sugar
2 cups sifted flour
8 eggs

Preheat the oven to 375°.

In a saucepan, combine the butter, water, salt, and sugar. Bring to a boil, and when the butter melts, add the flour all at once. Cook over low heat, beating constantly, until mixture forms a ball and leaves the sides of the pan. Remove from the heat and beat in 1 egg at a time. Continue beating until shiny and smooth.

To make cream puffs, drop from a teaspoon or tablespoon onto a greased baking pan, leaving 1 inch space between each. To make éclairs, force through a pastry tube into strips 4 inches long by 1 inch wide, or shape with 2 spoons. Bake small puffs (teaspoons) 30 minutes, or until puffy, browned, and free from moisture. Remove from oven, immediately cut slits in the sides, and return to oven for 5 minutes. Bake larger puffs (tablespoons) or éclairs 50 minutes. Slit and return to oven for 5 minutes. Cool on a cake rack; wrap, seal, label, and freeze the quantity you want, or fill with ice cream before freezing.

FOR IMMEDIATE SERVICE

Fill with ice cream, sweetened flavored whipped cream, etc., and serve with a chocolate or caramel sauce, if desired.

TO SERVE FROM FROZEN STATE

If unfilled, unwrap and place in a 325° oven for 10 minutes. Cool and fill as you like. If frozen with ice cream, remove from freezer 15 minutes before serving.

Makes about 60 small puffs or 24 large puffs or éclairs.

Note: The small puffs may also be used for hors d'oeuvres.

PUFF PASTE

    1 pound sweet butter
    4 cups flour
    1 teaspoon salt
    1 cup ice water

Knead the butter until smooth and waxlike and shape all but 4 tablespoons into a square ½ inch thick.

Sift the flour and salt into a bowl; work in the 4 tablespoons butter by hand. Add just enough of the water to make a ball of dough. On a lightly floured surface, roll out the dough into a rectangle ¼ inch thick. Place the butter in the center and fold over first one side and then the other, making 3 layers. Press the edges together and chill 15 minutes, wrapped in a damp cloth.

Place the dough on the lightly floured surface with the open end toward you. Using a chilled rolling pin, roll it out into a long rectangle. Fold into thirds again and turn so open end is toward you. Roll out, fold into thirds, wrap in the damp cloth, and chill 15 minutes. Repeat entire rolling process and chilling twice more. The dough is then ready to use as directed in recipes.

NAPOLEONS

Roll out the dough ⅛ inch thick and cut into 3 regular strips 3 inches wide by 10 inches long. Place on 3 foil-covered cardboards. Wrap, seal, label, and freeze.

FOR IMMEDIATE SERVICE

Place strips on a baking sheet and chill 30 minutes. Preheat oven to 450°. Bake 10 minutes, or until puffed. Reduce heat to 350° and bake 25 minutes longer, or until delicately browned. Cool and put the layers together with sweetened whipped cream. (Sliced strawberries may be folded into the cream.) Sprinkle top with confectioners' sugar.

TO SERVE FROM FROZEN STATE

Preheat oven to 450°.

Unwrap strips and arrange on a baking sheet. Bake 10 minutes, or until puffed. Reduce heat to 350° and bake 25 minutes longer, or until delicatedly browned. Fill as above.

Makes 2 10-inch 3-layered Napoleons.

PATTY SHELLS

Roll out puff paste ⅛ inch thick and cut into 3-inch circles. Lightly moisten the edges with cold water and put 3 together in layers. Cut a circular groove in the top layer ¾ inch from the edge. Place the number you want to freeze on a foil-covered cardboard. Wrap, seal, label, and freeze.

FOR IMMEDIATE SERVICE

Arrange on a baking sheet and chill 30 minutes. Preheat oven to 450°. Brush the tops with beaten egg yolk. Bake 5 minutes. Reduce heat to 350° and bake 20 minutes longer, or until delicately browned. Carefully lift out the centers; fill as you like and replace the center.

TO SERVE FROM FROZEN STATE

Preheat oven to 450°.

Unwrap the patty shells and place on a baking sheet. Brush with beaten egg yolk. Bake 5 minutes. Reduce heat to 350° and bake 20 minutes longer, or until delicately browned.

HOLIDAY COOKIES

⅜ pound (¾ cup) butter
1¼ cups sugar
1 egg
4 egg yolks
1 teaspoon vanilla extract
2 teaspoons grated lemon rind
3 cups sifted flour
⅛ teaspoon salt
3 tablespoons light cream
⅓ cup brown sugar
Almonds, candied cherries, or candied orange peel

Cream the butter, gradually adding the sugar. Beat until light and fluffy, then add the egg and egg yolks, vanilla, and lemon rind. Sift the flour and salt over the mixture gradually, stirring until well blended. Gather it into a ball, wrap in waxed paper, and chill overnight or for at least 4 hours.

Preheat oven to 400°. Roll out the dough as thin as possible on a lightly floured surface. Cut into circles, stars, or any shape you like. Transfer to cooky sheets with a spatula. Brush with the cream, sprinkle with brown sugar, and decorate with a half almond, cherry, or orange peel.

Bake about 7 minutes, or until delicately browned. Cool and pack into freezer containers with freezer paper between the layers.

If desired, you may bake only a small quantity for immediate use. Freeze the remaining rolled and decorated unbaked cookies on a baking sheet then pack into freezer containers with double layers of foil between the layers. Bake as directed when needed.

Makes about 6 dozen cookies.

FROZEN CHOCOLATE SOUFFLÉ

6 ounces sweet chocolate
4 tablespoons brewed coffee
6 whole eggs
6 egg yolks
2 cups sugar
3 envelopes (tablespoons) gelatin
4 tablespoons cold water
2 cups heavy cream

Melt the chocolate in the coffee.

Beat the eggs and egg yolks in the top of a double boiler with an electric mixer or rotary beater. Gradually add the sugar, beating until thick and light. Place over hot water and cook, stirring constantly, until mixture coats the spoon. Stir in the melted chocolate.

Soak the gelatin in the water for 5 minutes, then place over hot water and stir until dissolved. Add to the chocolate mixture; set aside until mixture begins to set. Beat with an electric mixer or rotary beater for 5 minutes.

Whip the cream and fold into the previous mixture.

Butter 2 long bands of waxed paper and tie around the tops of 2 1-quart buttered soufflé dishes, to form collars extending 3-4 inches over the tops of the dishes. Pour the mixture into the dishes (it should come up over the edges) and chill until set. Remove the paper collars. Wrap, seal, label, and freeze.

TO SERVE FROM FROZEN STATE

Remove from freezer 20 minutes before serving.

Serves 6–8 each time.

Note: If you don't have a soufflé dish, use a glass or pottery dish from which you can serve.

FROZEN LEMON SOUFFLÉ
Soufflé Glacé au Citron

2 envelopes (tablespoons) gelatin
½ cup cold water
12 egg yolks
2 cups sugar
1⅓ cups lemon juice
2 tablespoons grated lemon rind
8 egg whites, beaten stiff
3 cups heavy cream, whipped

Butter 2 bands of waxed paper and fasten around the tops of 2 1-quart buttered soufflé dishes to form collars extending 3–4 inches over the tops of the dishes.

Soften the gelatin in the water. Beat the egg yolks and sugar until thick and light. Stir in the lemon juice; cook over low heat, beating steadily, until mixture is thickened and coats the spoon. Mix in the gelatin until dissolved, and then the lemon rind. Remove from heat and cool, mixing occasionally.

Fold the egg whites, then the whipped cream into the lemon mixture. Slowly pour into the soufflé dishes. The mixture will rise above the top of the dish. Freeze, then carefully remove the paper collars. Wrap; seal, label, and return to freezer.

TO SERVE FROM FROZEN STATE

Unwrap dish, decorate top as above, and let stand in refrigerator for 3 hours before serving. Spread the top with whipped cream and decorate with lemon slices dipped in sugar.

Serves 8–10 each time.

FROZEN ORANGE SOUFFLÉ

3 envelopes (tablespoons) gelatin
1 cup orange juice
6 eggs
4 egg yolks
⅓ cup sugar
3 tablespoons grated orange rind
3 tablespoons curaçao or cointreau
2 cups heavy cream

Soften the gelatin in the orange juice. In the top of a double boiler, beat together the eggs, egg yolks, and sugar. Place over hot water and cook, stirring steadily, until thickened and pale in color. Stir in the gelatin until dissolved. Remove from the hot water and cool, stirring occasionally. Mix in the orange rind and liqueur. Whip the cream and fold into the orange mixture.

Butter 2 bands of waxed paper and tie around the tops of 2 1-quart buttered soufflé dishes to form collars extending 3–4 inches over the tops of the dishes. Divide the mixture between them; the mixture should rise 2 inches above the top of the dish. Chill; wrap carefully, label, and freeze.

TO SERVE FROM FROZEN STATE

Remove dish from freezer 3 hours before serving. Unwrap and carefully remove the paper collar. Dissolve 2 tablespoons currant jelly in 2 tablespoons curaçao or cointreau; brush the top with it. Refrigerate for 1 hour to set jelly.

Serves 6–8 each time.

RASPBERRY MOUSSE

2 envelopes (tablespoons) gelatin
1 cup cold water
4 packages frozen raspberries
½ cup sugar
4 egg whites
3 cups heavy cream

Soften the gelatin in the water.

Drain the berries thoroughly and measure the juice. If necessary, add water to make 2 cups. Combine the juice and sugar in a saucepan; cook over low heat until syrupy. Add the berries; cook over low heat 10 minutes. Mix in the gelatin until dissolved. Force through a sieve. Cool.

Beat the egg whites until stiff but not dry. Fold into the raspberry mixture. Whip the cream lightly and add; beat the mixture until thick. Pour into 2 1½–quart molds and chill until set. Wrap 1; seal, label, and freeze.

FOR IMMEDIATE SERVICE

Decorate the top with cognac-flavored whipped cream and whole raspberries.

TO SERVE FROM FROZEN STATE

Remove from freezer 3 hours before serving. Unwrap and decorate as above, if desired. Let stand in refrigerator until ready to serve.

Serves 6–8 each time.

LEMON CHEESE

    2 envelopes (tablespoons) gelatin
    1 cup lemon juice
    7 eggs
    8 egg yolks
    1½ cups sugar
    4 tablespoons grated lemon rind
    6 cups heavy cream

Soften the gelatin in the lemon juice; place over hot water and stir until dissolved.

Beat the eggs and yolks; gradually add the sugar, beating until light and fluffy. Stir in the gelatin with the rind. Whip the cream and fold in. Divide among 3 1-quart soufflé dishes or containers. Chill; wrap, label, and freeze.

FOR IMMEDIATE SERVICE
    Chill 4 hours.

TO SERVE FROM FROZEN STATE
    Remove from freezer 1 hour before serving time, or place in refrigerator 4 hours before.
    Serves 6–8 each time.

COGNAC CREAM

8 egg yolks
½ cup sugar
¾ cup cognac
6 egg whites, stiffly beaten
2 cups heavy cream, whipped

In the top of a double boiler, beat the egg yolks and sugar. Place over hot water and cook, stirring steadily, until frothy and hot; do not let boil. Remove from heat and stir in the cognac. Cool. Fold in the egg whites and then the whipped cream. Turn into 2 1½-quart molds; cover, wrap, seal, label, and freeze until needed.

TO SERVE FROM FROZEN STATE
Unwrap mold and dip in hot water for a few seconds. Turn out onto a chilled serving dish and place in refrigerator for a few minutes.

Serves 8–10 each time.

ICE CREAM

VANILLA
1 cup milk
4 cups heavy cream
8 egg yolks
1 cup sugar
1½ teaspoons vanilla extract

Bring to a boil the milk and 3 cups cream. Beat the egg yolks and sugar in a saucepan (with a whisk or fork) until smooth and thickened. Gradually add the hot cream mixture, stirring steadily to prevent curdling. Cook over very low heat, still stirring steadily until thickened, but do not let boil. Stir in the vanilla. If there are any lumps, strain the mixture. Chill, turn into 2 ice trays, and freeze until sides become mushy.

Turn into a bowl and beat until smooth and frothy. Return to trays until almost frozen and beat again. Whip the remaining cream and fold in. Return to trays, freeze again. Wrap the trays until needed.

Serves 6–8.

CHOCOLATE
Add 3 ounces melted semisweet chocolate to the yolk mixture. Proceed as directed.

COFFEE-COGNAC
2 tablespoons instant coffee
2 tablespoons boiling water
4 tablespoons cognac

Dissolve the coffee in the water. Reduce milk to ½ cup. Add coffee and cognac with cream mixture. Proceed as directed.

STRAWBERRY OR RASPBERRY
Add 1 cup crushed berries to the yolk mixture. Proceed as directed.

218 COOKING FOR THE FREEZER

CHOCOLATE LIQUEUR BOMBE

1½ cups sugar
1 cup water
8 egg yolks
1 quart heavy cream
3 tablespoons cognac or orange liqueur
1 quart chocolate ice cream

Boil the sugar and water together for 5 minutes. Beat the egg yolks in the top of a double boiler; gradually add the hot syrup, stirring steadily to prevent curdling. Cook over hot water, stirring steadily, until mixture coats the spoon. Remove from the hot water and cool over ice, stirring frequently.

Whip the cream and fold it into the previous mixture with the liqueur. Line 2 1½–quart bombe or other molds with the chocolate ice cream. Freeze for a few minutes. Turn the cream mixture into them; cover, wrap, label, and freeze.

TO SERVE FROM FROZEN STATE

Remove from freezer 1 hour before needed. Unwrap, dip mold in hot water for a few seconds, and carefully turn out. Return to freezer until ready to serve.

Serves 8–10 each time.

SPUMONE

10 egg yolks
2 cups sugar
4 cups light cream, scalded
2 teaspoons vanilla extract
2 ounces semisweet chocolate, melted
2 cups heavy cream
4 tablespoons chopped candied fruit
2 tablespoons cognac

Beat the egg yolks and 1½ cups sugar in a saucepan until thick and light. Gradually add the hot cream, stirring steadily to prevent curdling. Cook over low heat, stirring steadily, until mixture coats the spoon; do not let boil. Remove from heat and stir in the vanilla. Transfer 2 cups of the mixture to a small bowl and blend in the chocolate. Cool both mixtures, then freeze until they hold their shape.

Line 2 1-quart spumone or melon molds with the vanilla mixture. Freeze for a few minutes, then spread chocolate mixture over it. Freeze for a few minutes. Whip the cream and fold in the fruit, cognac, and remaining sugar. Fill the centers of the molds. Cover with a piece of waxed paper; wrap, seal, label, and freeze.

TO SERVE FROM FROZEN STATE

Dip mold in hot water for a few seconds, then carefully turn out onto a chilled serving dish. Cut with a silver knife dipped in hot water.

Serves 6–8 each time.

PEARS IN PORT

1½ cups port wine
1½ cups sugar
¼ teaspoon cinnamon
2 slivers lemon rind
12 pears
3 tablespoons cognac

Bring the wine, sugar, cinnamon, and lemon rind to a boil. Peel the pears and arrange in the mixture. Cook over low heat until pears are tender but firm. Remove the pears. Cook the syrup until reduced to half. Cool. Stir in the cognac.

Pack the pears and syrup into containers in quantities suitable for serving. Seal, label, and freeze.

TO SERVE FROM FROZEN STATE

Remove container from freezer 2 hours before serving.

BISCUIT TORTONI

2 cups heavy cream
2 egg whites
½ cup sugar
2 tablespoons sweet sherry
¾ cup ground almonds

Whip the cream. Beat the egg whites until stiff; gradually beat in the sugar. Fold in the whipped cream with the sherry and ½ cup of the almonds. Spoon into 12 3-ounce paper cups. Sprinkle the remaining almonds on top. Freeze, then pack in freezer containers. Return to freezer until ready to serve.

MELON BALLS

1½ cups sugar
3 cups water
12 cups melon balls

Bring the sugar and water to a boil and cook until sugar melts.
Chill.

You may use canteloupe, watermelon, honeydew, or any other
type of melon, singly or mixed. If you don't want to make balls,
peel, remove seeds, and cube. Pack into pint or quart containers
and cover with the syrup. Seal, label, and freeze.

TO SERVE FROM FROZEN STATE

Remove container from freezer 3–4 hours before serving. Keep
covered at room temperature until thawed but still firm

Makes 3 quarts.

COFFEE ICE
Granite de Café

2 cups sugar
2 cups water
6 cups cold, double-strength coffee

Boil the sugar and water together for 5 minutes. Cool; mix with the coffee. Pour into a freezer tray and freeze without stirring until granular but not solid. Cover with foil or freezer paper until needed.
Serves 12.

CHOCOLATE ICES

1 cup chocolate syrup
¼ cup sugar
1 quart water
1½ teaspoons almond extract
1 teaspoon powdered cinnamon

Beat together all the ingredients in a bowl. Place in the freezer until sides set. Beat with a rotary beater until frothy. Freeze again.
Makes about 1½ quarts.

CARE OF THE FREEZER

Freezers and refrigerator-freezer combinations require special care, as some models are not equipped with an automatic defroster. It is a good idea to clean the freezer thoroughly and completely at least once a year, even if it is self-defrosting. In regions with high humidity, three or even four times a year may be desirable if it isn't self-defrosting. You will have to be the judge, as each appliance operates somewhat differently in varying climatic conditions.

When the frost in the freezer is about ¼ inch thick, and dropping off in the form of snow onto the packages, it is time to do a thorough cleaning. In between times, scrape off accumulated frost with a plastic scraper, the kind used by motorists to remove snow and ice from the windshield. Work carefully so as not to damage the finish.

Before defrosting, remove all frozen foods and wrap in several thicknesses of paper (newspapers, etc.) to prevent thawing. If you have a separate refrigerator, place the wrapped foods in it. Defrost the freezer; place pans of hot water in it to speed the defrosting process. Sop up accumulated water with sponges. Remove large pieces of frost with a scraper, but don't use an ice pick or other sharp instrument, because you might accidentally damage the freezing mechanism.

Don't begin cleaning the freezer until it is completely defrosted. Wash the interior with lukewarm water, mixed with a little baking soda. Afterward rinse with clean water and dry thoroughly. Set the freezer dial at its highest (coldest) point. Replace the foods; discard those foods that may have been overlooked and kept in storage for too long a time. Reset freezer dial to its customary position after 4 hours.

Keep a file of the dishes you have frozen, so as not to forget what you have on hand. Delicious preparations may be overlooked or forgotten, as time goes by, unless you maintain an inventory record.

INDEX